# SCANDINAVIA

## JOHN H. WUORINEN

A SPECTRUM BOOK

Prentice-Hall, Inc.

*Englewood Cliffs, New Jersey*

This survey of Scandinavia deals mostly with the twentieth century; only two of its ten chapters summarize historical developments and related matters before World War I. Four chapters (except for the chapter on Iceland) are devoted to the quarter-century since the Hitler-Stalin pact of August 23, 1939, and the invasion of Poland a week later. Two other chapters—Chapters Four and Five—also deal primarily with the recent past or the more or less contemporary scene, although somewhat earlier periods are also discussed.

The fact that the survey covers five nations—Denmark, Finland, Iceland, Norway, and Sweden—rather than one, dictated an approach and organization that in many respects accents broad homogeneities rather than differences. This approach could be used without sacrificing essentials because the nations are similar in many ways. Yet within the broad categories used in sketching the developments since 1914, the individual states and peoples frequently stand out in clear relief. The sharpness of national contours is determined by the decisive facts in each case. "Scandinavian economy," for instance, is an abstraction that becomes a meaningful generalization only if and when the underpinnings of the generalization, the economies of the individual nations, are properly identified. And it is of course clear that until real political unity in the North becomes a reality—a far from likely possibility in the foreseeable future—a discussion of constitutions, parliaments, politics, and the like must move almost wholly within the separate concerns of each nation. Similarly, questions of foreign policy cannot be meaningfully discussed without clarifying national rather than "Scandinavian" interests and purposes. (Iceland stands, geographically and in other ways, sufficiently apart from the other Northern countries to require description as a separate national and political entity.) Thus broad homogeneities must frequently yield, as the component parts of this survey illustrate, to par-

v

ticulars defined by the past history and present circumstances of each nation.

In writing the book, I have placed myself under a heavy obligation to the authors of many special studies and general works. The bibliography, limited to publications in English, lists some of them. I would also like to record my indebtedness to the students in my Scandinavian History course at Columbia University, and especially to my wife, for generous assistance during every phase of the preparation of this book.

J.H.W.

# CONTENTS

# SCANDINAVIA

# ONE

# THE LANDS AND THE PEOPLES

Before World War I, American awareness of the peoples of Scandinavia was limited largely to those who had emigrated to the United States in search of opportunities and rewards greater than those offered in their homelands. Although the first contacts with America that might be called Scandinavian had been made by Icelanders centuries before Columbus sailed the ocean blue, they remained wholly without influence. Permanent Scandinavian roots in the New World were put down by a handful of Swedes and Finns in 1638, when the New Sweden colony was founded on the Delaware. (New Sweden was taken by the Dutch in 1654.) But the Scandinavian settlers at no time numbered more than a few hundred souls, and the colony itself remained small and unimportant. By the mid-eighteenth century, English had become the language of all—or nearly all—those who might still be considered Swedes or Finns.

It was only in the nineteenth century that the Scandinavian lands began to make significant contributions to the broadening stream of immigration to the New World. By 1850, about 20,000 Scandinavians had reached the United States. Some 13,000 of this number came from Norway, and about 4000 from Sweden; the Danes and the Finns came in much smaller numbers.

The next half-century considerably changed the picture. In 1900, Scandinavian immigrants in the United States numbered approximately 1.1 million—almost 10 per cent of the total population of Scandinavia at the time (12.3 million), though only a small fraction of the United States' total of 76 million. It has been estimated that by 1950 the four nations of the North had contributed about 2.5 million newcomers to the population of the United States: the largest number—1.1 million—came from Sweden; Norway contributed 815,000; Finland, some 400,000; and Denmark, 340,000. The majority of these immigrants settled in Minnesota, Michigan, Wisconsin, the

Dakotas, Iowa, Nebraska, Illinois, Massachusetts, New York, and the Pacific Coast states. By 1920—the last census year before the restrictive immigration legislation of the 1920's—descendants of Swedish and Norwegian stock constituted the largest ethnic groups in all these states (except Michigan, where the Finnish element was somewhat larger than the others).[1]

During the past few decades, American interest in the Scandinavian peoples has increased, primarily because of their political, social, and foreign policies—especially during the East-West Cold War. About fifteen years ago Sumner Welles suggested that Americans should become familiar with the Scandinavian's history and life in general, especially because "we have so much to learn from every one of the Scandinavian countries in the science of democratic government." He went on to say that "Scandinavian social democracy [did he mean socialism?] offers a comforting proof that men occasionally can govern themselves wisely and well." [2]

Understandable as this interest is—and however flattering to the Scandinavians—it is likely to be and to remain sterile if it implies that the Scandinavian formulas are applicable to our own political and economic problems. The plain fact is that although the nations of the North have been surprisingly successful in providing for their own needs and in solving their own problems—needs and problems often no less complex than those of the larger nations—they have not discovered (nor do they claim to have discovered) principles or systems appropriate for export. Scandinavian "democratic self-government" is likely to offer an American observer little beyond a few obvious conclusions.

Perhaps the outstanding among these conclusions is that certain qualities—hard work, stern common sense, a largely unassailable honesty in public life, a long tradition in what is often and at times rather glibly spoken of as self-government or democratic processes, great stress on education, and a more than moderate capacity for maintaining a disciplined social order and for cultivating the arts of compromise essential for reasonable political tranquillity—are basic reasons for the Scandinavians' success in the difficult business of self-rule.

---

[1] *Historical Statistics of the United States, 1789-1945* (Washington, D.C.: USGPO, 1949), tables on pp. 33-35. I am indebted, for some of the figures, to my colleague Professor Robert D. Cross. See also Franklin D. Scott, *The United States and Scandinavia* (Cambridge, Mass.: Harvard University Press, 1940), map on p. 71.

[2] Scott, *op. cit.*, p.x.

Because the past history and the present economic, political, and social circumstances of Scandinavia suggest that life in these small countries is in many ways no less complex than that in the larger democracies of the Western world, it is easier to understand the mysteries of the human condition in the North, and to see in the life and accomplishment of these free peoples not only a fascinating fragment of history worth reflective study for its own sake, but a meaningful and challenging commentary on man.

### The Lands: Climate and Resources

Historians and others have often remarked that Denmark, Finland, Norway, and Sweden constitute a markedly homogeneous unit, sharply contrasting with the rest of western Europe. The similarity of their political institutions derives from the fact that all four nations are genuine democracies (although three of them are monarchies and only one is a republic). In each, the freedom and liberties of the individual citizen furnish the solid foundation upon which government rests. The economic development of the Scandinavian nations has followed much the same general pattern—one that prominently accents private enterprise and not "a planned domestic economy," as Marquis W. Childs[3] and many others have contended. This pattern was impressively emphasized at the New York World's Fair in 1964, where the slogan of the Swedish Pavilion was "Creative Sweden—Land of Free Enterprise." The slogan would, in fact, apply to all four Scandinavian countries. Common features are equally evident in the position and role of the national churches—overwhelmingly Lutheran—and the goals and purposes of educational institutions. The corpus of law and the administration of justice also disclose common principles and procedures in regulating the complicated business of man's life in society.

These facts alone make it clear that Scandinavia describes a group of nations among which there exists a degree of homogeneity unique in Europe. This is in a sense surprising, for these nations are no minuscule entities or tiny political units forced by their insignificance to seek strength and security by cultivating the art of cooperation. The four nations comprise an area of about 445,500 square miles: Denmark, 16,500; Finland, 130,100; Norway, 124,560; and Sweden, the largest of the four, 173,350. Their total area, in European terms is quite large: it is nearly five times the area of the United Kingdom, more than twice the size of France, over four times the size of West Germany,

[3] Marquis W. Childs, Harper's Magazine (November 1933).

and well over three and a half times the size of Italy. Finland alone is almost half again as large as the United Kingdom, while Sweden is nearly twice the size of West Germany. Scandinavia covers an area equal to that of the New England states, New York, New Jersey, Pennsylvania, Ohio, Indiana, Illinois, Michigan, and Wisconsin combined.

The four countries vary greatly in size and configuration. Denmark, the smallest, is really a huge archipelago. The land frontier in the south is only forty-two miles long, while the coast line runs for about 4600 miles. A low and undulating plain, Denmark's highest point is only 568 feet above sea level. No more than 10 per cent of its area is covered by forests, while some three quarters is cultivated agricultural acreage improved by centuries of intelligent tillage.

Denmark still has two overseas possessions that represent the last of more extensive earlier dependencies: Greenland, with an area of about 840,000 square miles and a population (as of 1959) of 30,600; and the Faroe Islands, with an area of 540 square miles and a population of about 34,000. (Iceland, formerly a part of the Danish domain, was granted home rule in 1903 and independence—though still in union with Denmark, under a common king—in 1918. It was declared a republic in 1944.)

Finland, Norway, and Sweden differ conspicuously from Denmark not only in size—they are about eight to ten times as large—but in other important respects as well. Nearly all of Finland is relatively low: most of it is less than 600 feet above sea level; areas in the north and east reach a height of only about 1500 feet, and the highest mountain in the far northwest is under 5000 feet. The country, however, offers a good deal of variety. Both the southern and western coastal regions of Finland are fringed by an extensive belt of islands. Tens of thousands of lakes—accounting for about one tenth of the country's area—and countless rivers cover much of central Finland. Except for the western coastal plain and the southwest, the extensive forests seem all too often to crowd in upon the open farming lands. Nevertheless, the forests have furnished, for the greater part of the past century, the most important single basis for the industrial structure of the nation.

Norway stands in a category by itself. Long and narrow—its greatest width is under 300 miles and its narrowest only four miles—Norway covers the western part of the Scandinavian peninsula, for a distance of well over 1000 miles as the crow flies. It is a mountainous country; its average altitude is nearly twice that of Europe in general, and only one fifth of it lies lower than 200 feet above sea level. Furrowed by many valleys, traversed by rivers, dotted with lakes large and small, its coast line indented by numerous fjords, its mountainous upland regions reaching as high as 8000 feet, Norway is indeed most richly endowed.

Sweden's 173,350 square miles place her among the largest countries in Europe. The climate varies a good deal: below-freezing temperatures occur, on an average, only fifty-six days a year in the south, but 217 days a year in the far north. Only some twelve per cent of the population lives in the northern half of the country. It is in the north, however, that the greater part of Sweden's extensive forest resources and valuable ore deposits are located. Iron ore of exceptional purity heads the list, which also includes copper, silver, and gold. The plains in the central and southern parts of the country sustain a flourishing agriculture which importantly supplements the industrial economy that has become the hallmark of twentieth-century Sweden. Much of western Sweden is dominated by the high mountain range that separates her from Norway.

By no stretch of the imagination could these countries be considered colonial powers. Two of them, however—Denmark and Norway—have dependencies or possessions overseas. Mention has already been made of Denmark's holdings. Norway's domain includes Svalbard (or Spitsbergen) in the Arctic Ocean, a number of islands that formally became part of the kingdom of Norway in 1925. In 1929 Norway acquired Jan Mayen island in the Norwegian Sea; it was fully incorporated as a part of the kingdom in 1930. Three Antarctic possessions—Bouvet Island, Peter I Island, and Queen Maud Land on the Antarctic coast—complete the list of Norwegian dependencies.

Geography divides rather than unites the four countries. The immutable verdict of geography places Denmark, in a sense, outside Scandinavia proper. The northern arm of the Baltic Sea, the Gulf of Bothnia, separates most of Finland from Sweden. It is therefore clear that only Norway and Sweden constitute, in a geographical sense, "Scandinavia." But a closer look at the map discloses the fact that these, too, are separated. Along the whole length of the Scandinavian peninsula there runs the spine of a mountain range, the Kölen, that cuts it in two and accounts for the fact that, as many have put it, Sweden faces east while Norway faces west. The divisive consequences of the mountain range have begun to diminish with improvements in methods of travel and communication.

A glance at the map of Europe suffices to show the marked geographical separateness of the Scandinavian lands from the rest of western Europe. Denmark's forty-two-mile land frontier with Germany is Scandinavia's only "European" border. Since the defeat of Hitlerite Germany in World War II, and so long as the present international situation in western Europe continues, the short Danish-German border exposes neither Denmark nor Scandinavia as a whole to the threat of aggression or war from the south. Scandinavia's eastern borders, on the other hand, represent a more ominous reality. Cold War frictions have emphasized the differences of the worlds east and west of the Scandinavian-Soviet boundaries. These boundaries involve only two of the four nations: Norway, whose Soviet border is 122 miles long, and Finland, whose Soviet border runs for 720 miles. The Norwegian and Finnish boundaries with the Soviet Union mark off, probably more sharply than anywhere else in Europe, the world of Western freedoms and democracy from the pretensions and practices of Moscow-led Communism.

Within Scandinavia itself, national boundaries stand out in significant and reassuring contrast. Norway's boundary with Sweden is 1000 miles long; its boundary with Finland runs 447 miles. Finland's boundary with Sweden is 335 miles long. The divisive effect of these boundaries has been largely eliminated, particularly during the last decade or two, by agreements and arrangements that have created new and intimate good-neighbor relationships among the four nations. The citizens of any one of the four nations no longer need passports to travel anywhere else in Scandinavia. Customs and currency controls at these frontiers have been eliminated, and an international Scandinavian labor market was established in 1954, when work permits were reciprocally abolished by Denmark, Finland, Norway, and Sweden. Unique as these evidences of international cooperation are, they are only part of a larger and expanding pattern that has emerged in Scandinavia, especially since the end of World War II.

The natural resources of these northern lands are far from abundant. The climate, to be sure, is milder than the latitude suggests. It is far from benign but, except for some mountain areas in northern Norway and Sweden, there are neither glaciers nor permanent snow and frost. Elsewhere in Scandinavia the climate is tempered by the Gulf Stream. Hundreds of miles wide and several hundred yards deep, the Gulf Stream runs northward along the western coast of Norway and then eastward into the Barents Sea. It keeps the cold Polar waters deep in the Arctic Sea and gives rise to warm, moist air currents. Thus the mean January temperature along Norway's western coast is well over twenty degrees higher than the mean temperature for the latitude; in southwest Finland, the mean temperature of the coldest month, February, ranges from 19° to 28°F. (and, in the far North, from 12° to −5°F.). Denmark, being considerably farther south, has a natural advantage accented by the Gulf Stream: the average temperature in the coldest month is some twelve degrees higher than the latitude would lead one to expect. Even Denmark, however, annually experiences freezing weather for periods that range from seventy days in the coastal areas to 120 days in the interior. The long days during the growing season compensate, to a surprising degree, for the absence of really warm weather, because the transpiration of water through plants, essential for the growth of vegetation, proceeds only during daylight. In Norway, north of the Arctic Circle, for example, the intense sun and long days mean that barley ripens in about sixty days, while the ripening process requires almost 100 days in the southern part of the country. Thus, although the expression "the lands of the midnight sun" is something of an exaggeration when applied to the Scandinavian states, they do enjoy an exceptional abundance of daylight during the summer months.

Nor has Nature been overgenerous in providing soil, another fundamental requisite for life in general and for farming in particular. Arable land is rather unevenly distributed in Scandinavia. Denmark is more abundantly supplied with good farming acreage than Norway, Sweden, or Finland. Almost 75 per cent of Denmark's area is agricultural land. In Norway, the cultivated area is only 3 per cent of the total; in Finland, about 10 per cent; and in Sweden, approximately 9 per cent. This does not mean that agriculture no longer plays a significant part in the national economies of these countries. The surprising efficiency and importance of agriculture results from the widespread utilization of techniques offered by expert soil chemistry, successful breeding of hardy varieties of grain—in Finland, barley, oats, and rye are grown well north of the Arctic Circle—hard work, and (especially in recent decades) extensive use of modern farm machinery.

Niggardly as Nature has been in some respects, it has been generous in others. The major part of Finland, Sweden, and Norway is covered by extensive forests. Modern technological advances have transformed the forest lands, once an obstacle to man's progress and prosperity, into a most valuable asset. Scientific forestry techniques have made of the forests a self-perpetuating source of wealth upon which rests a large part of the industrial economy of modern Scandinavia: paper, pulp, prefabricated housing, and a wide variety of wood products ranging from veneers to furniture and from pit props to matches testify to the broad sector of industry sustained by the "green gold" of Scandinavia's forests. Not the least impressive commentary on Danish ingenuity is the fact that Denmark's forest areas, which a century and a half ago had shrunk—because of mismanagement and lack of foresight—to some 4 per cent of the total area of the country, today account for about 10 per cent of the total acreage and furnish nearly half of the nation's annual timber needs.

Nature has also endowed the Scandinavian countries (except Denmark) with important water-power resources. Because these countries have no coal or oil,[4] their energy needs have increasingly depended upon water power. Norway and Sweden are most favored in this regard. Although Norway's water-power sites are unevenly distributed, most of them are located in the southwestern part of the country. The falls are close to deep, ice-free fjords and are therefore well suited to industrial exploitation. The potential annual capacity of these resources was estimated, in 1956, at 12.5 trillion kilowatt-hours. In 1962, Sweden's hydroelectric power plants produced about 42 billion kilowatt-hours; Norway's, 37.74 billion; and Finland's, 11.1 billion.[5]

Nature has also bestowed valuable mineral resources upon the Northern lands. Sweden's iron ore deposits are among the richest in the world, and Norway's are also significant. Other ores and metals of industrial importance—such as copper, zinc, silver, and gold— are also found. Even Denmark, which lacks water power, oil, and iron or other mineral resources, has huge clay and lime deposits (these furnish the basis of a significant cement industry), silicon, and—in Greenland—cryolite.

As can be seen, the Scandinavians' high standard of culture and living could not have emerged solely from their own resources of soil

---

[4] Modest lignite (brown coal) deposits are found in southern Sweden but they are of small significance. The value of the output in 1962 came to some $600,000. Norway has mined coal in Svalbard for many years; the tonnage was 403,600 in 1960, 369,000 in 1961, and 445,500 in 1962. Somewhat over one third of the coal is shipped to Norway; the rest is sold abroad. (Statements by the Swedish Information Service and the Norwegian Information Service, New York, January 12 and 13, 1965.)

[5] United Nations Statistical Yearbook, 1963, Table 132, pp. 343-45. Table 45, p. 169, gives Sweden's coal production in 1962 as 139,000 tons and Norway's (Svalbard's) as 444,000 tons.

or climate. Something else has been, and remains, an indispensable condition for their continued prosperity and progress. That something else is foreign trade. Deprived of the opportunities and benefits of international trade, the peoples of the North could probably have produced the bare essentials of a meager life, but they could not possibly have attained the high levels of prosperity recorded during the past half-century. This is merely one way of saying that the growing volume and diversity of their trade with the outside world has enabled them to benefit from the international division of labor made possible by the general economic development since the closing decades of the 1800's. As a result of this international division of labor, and of the industrialization that has both caused and been caused by it, foreign trade has become indispensable to the Scandinavians. Their way of life could not possibly be maintained without a large and continuing pattern of exports and imports. Neither the industrial nor the agricultural sectors of their economies could function in the manner that has come to be considered as normal and desirable without a continuous outflow of industrial and agricultural products and a continuous inflow of raw materials, coal, oil, lubricants, foods, feeds, fertilizers, automobiles, machinery, appliances, and a large number of other commodities indispensable to modern industrial, urban societies.

Because the Scandinavian nations are, in a sense, islands, their dependence on foreign trade involves a situation and a common problem frequently overlooked: most of their foreign markets can be reached only by ship. Overland foreign commercial exchange is, on the whole, of only secondary importance (although it is clear that Denmark, for example, is more favorably situated in this regard than Finland, Norway, or Sweden). Scandinavian economies are, therefore, largely dependent upon the uninterrupted shipping of exports and imports. Thus autarchic policies, international crises, and war unavoidably have a retarding or outright destructive effect upon the economies of these nations. This is a basic reason for modern Scandinavia's policy of peace and neutrality.

### The Peoples: Origins and Characteristics

In terms of population, the Scandinavian nations do not rank high. The combined populations came to no more than 20.3 million in 1960. Sweden headed the list with 7.5 million, Denmark followed with 4.6 million, and Finland with 4.5 million, while Norway brought up the rear with 3.6 million. The total falls far short of half the population figures for each of the following: Italy, France, West Germany, and the United Kingdom. Spain and Poland each exceeds Scandinavia's population figure by some 10 million. In the United States, New York State alone has a population that is approximately 80 per cent of all Scandinavia's.

The population growth of the four nations during the past two centuries is shown in Table I (Sweden and Finland's population statistics go back to 1749; Denmark's and Norway's, to 1769).

TABLE I

SCANDINAVIA'S POPULATION, 1750-1960

|  | Denmark | Finland | Norway | Sweden |
|---|---|---|---|---|
| 1750 | 760,000 | 421,000 | 720,000 | 1,800,000 |
| 1800 | 920,000 | 832,000 | 880,000 | 2,300,000 |
| 1850 | 1,400,000 | 1,624,000 | 1,400,000 | 3,500,000 |
| 1900 | 2,400,000 | 2,656,000 | 2,200,000 | 5,100,000 |
| 1950 | 4,300,000 | 4,030,000 | 3,279,000 | 6,600,000 |
| 1960 | 4,650,000 | 4,550,000 | 3,650,000 | 7,500,000 |

The physical characteristics of the Scandinavians are usually described in terms that have become almost cliché: they are tall, blond, blue- or gray-eyed, fair-skinned people. The anthropological facts that furnish the basis for the descriptions rest on government records of the measurements of army recruits and, occasionally, on more detailed local studies. An official Norwegian compilation, published in 1962, provides the average height of recruits: Norwegian, 172.4 centimeters; Swedish, 172.2; Finnish, 171.1; and Danish, 169.5. (All of these come to less than five feet eight inches.) A Swedish publication devoted to a study of "Swedish folk types," published in 1919 by the Race Biological Institute in Stockholm, held that 10.7 per cent of the Swedes are "pure Nordics"; tall stature, one of the characteristics of this type, was defined as 170 centimeters (about five feet seven inches) or over. Obviously, if *tall* were defined as, say, six feet, the percentage of "pure Nordics" would sharply decrease.

Whatever the conclusions regarding stature, complexion, color of hair or skin, cranial index, or facial angles, the meaningful facts are obvious: the physical similarities among these peoples are strong. The differences are much smaller between nations than within each individual nation. In Norway and Finland, for example, the stature of the population in the northern areas is markedly lower than that of the population in the south (partly, perhaps, because of the admixture of the Lapp element). Norway's western and southwestern districts have a population considerably shorter and darker than that in the southeast. The western and southern areas of Finland show the tallest and blondest types; black hair and brown or dark eyes are rare in the country as a whole. Denmark and Sweden illustrate, in varying degree, similar differences. The explanation for the differences appears to be an ancient cross-breeding of different races or types. Since the dawn of recorded history, however, these peoples have remained almost untouched by the influx of newcomers.

This insularity is one of the factors underlying the homogeneity of the Scandinavian populations today. Foreign linguistic or ethnic elements are altogether insignificant. One of them is the Lapps: today there are about 20,000 in Norway, 7000 in Sweden, and 2500 in Finland. The Jews, who in no sense represent an ethnic or "racial" problem in these lands, are also small in numbers: 1500 in Finland, 7000 in Sweden, 9000 in Denmark, and 2500 in Norway. Thus none of these nations has the racial or minority problems which have plagued many other parts of Europe.

The problem of the Finns' racial origins is more complicated than that of most other European peoples. Linguistically, they are an almost completely isolated people, although Estonian is close enough to Finnish to enable even a layman to see the relationship. Hungarian is often mentioned as another language related to Finnish, but the relationship is discernible only to trained philologists; actually the relationship is about as close as that between English and Persian or, say, Swedish and Persian. It sufficed, however, through much of the nineteenth century and well into the twentieth, to sustain and perpetuate the idea that the racial antecedents of the Finns corresponded to the linguistic connections delineated by philologists.

Before modern race studies worthy of the name appeared, speech was generally accepted as the criterion of race and nationality. In recent decades, however, scientists have agreed that language, as a criterion of race, is often meaningless—whether applied to Europeans in general or to Scandinavians in particular. However hard to define, race is a biological fact; language, on the other hand, is a so-called cultural product derived from human experience and influenced by historical evolution. It can be, and often is, changed. Racial boundaries seldom fully correspond to linguistic boundaries; no matter how they are drawn, they do not give us a clear picture of the bewildering—and probably unknowable—combination of racial origins. They fail to tell us how today's races came to be that which, in time, they will probably cease to be.

It was the older theory that led to the conclusion that the Finns should be classified with certain Asian peoples whose languages, it was contended, belonged in the same category as Finnish (the so-called Ural-Altaic concept). That these conclusions were partly formulated and largely popularized by Finnish nineteenth-century scholars and nationalists intent on proving, among other things, the relationship of their nation with a sizable part of the world's population, helped to solidify these notions. Ultimately they became relatively impervious to the challenge of later scientists whose studies of race in general or of the physical characteristics of the Finns in particular should have sufficed to render a verdict quite different from that originally put forth by romanticizing philologist-patriots and their followers.

The verdict is that the Finns today, and their recognizable forebears in historic times, are "purely European." The distant origins of the Finns, like those of other European peoples, are hidden—and, in all likelihood, will ever remain hidden—in the impenetrable darkness of the past. The place of the Finns among the other peoples of the North, or of Europe as a whole, can be defined in only one way: according to the readily available facts regarding the Finns' physical characteristics. These facts place the Finns where their whole recorded history has placed them over the centuries: in the same category with the other Northern peoples.

Although the homogeneity of the Scandinavian peoples is obvious to any serious observer, it by no means obscures important national differences. The differences rest upon and grow out of several factors and circumstances.

It appears safe to say that the intangibles that distinguish, say, the Danes or the Finns from the Swedes or the Norwegians are not the result of geography or of race. The Dane or the Finn or the Norwegian or the Swede is more the product of historical, human, and cultural forces and influences than of the physical environment in which he lives. It is in accepted modes of thought, in ways of perceiving and interpreting the past of his country, in the content and meaning of patriotism—that transcends, especially in times of national crisis, party, social, and regional differences—that the Dane or the Norwegian stands out among his fellow Scandinavians. It is his national tradition and what it implies that enables the Finn or the Swede to experience emotional responses to many aspects of his country's history or his nation's achievements that leave the foreigner indifferent. It also makes it possible—perhaps mandatory—for him to devote his deepest patriotic loyalties to his own country and to no other. It is the strong feeling of national consciousness, its taproots in the past and its manifold consequences in more recent times, that deprive the Scandinavian area as a whole of what might be called, for want of a better term, a common mainstream of historical experience. This accounts, in the main, for the marked differences between Sweden-Finland on the one hand, and Denmark-Norway on the other, before the nineteenth century and for the more sharply defined Northern nationality concepts and lines of demarcation of the twentieth. That the enrichment and perpetuation of each national tradition in Scandinavia has been carried on, especially during the past half-century, with only minimal friction or ill will is one of the most significant aspects of the history of the North.

# TWO

# HISTORY:

## TRENDS AND CONSEQUENCES

### Before the Rise of the National State

Historians of Scandinavia frequently mention ancient writers—Arabs, Greeks, and Romans—who described or commented on that faraway northern land and its peoples long before its own recorded history begins. Outstanding among them is Tacitus, whose *Germania* (98 A.D.) has often been cited as a source of meaningful information. His designation of the peoples or tribes of the North makes it possible to identify, after a fashion, the Swedes and the Finns as well as the Danes and the Norwegians.

Tacitus was neither a traveler nor a geographer; he had never visited the areas he described. He is generally considered to have based his accounts on a careful study of materials available to him and on the statements and descriptions made by travelers whom he consulted. His descriptions of Scandinavia and the peoples of the North are brief and extremely generalized. The meager details he gives are either pointless, trivial, or—in the absence of any proof—incredible. They are, for all practical purposes, meaningless and leave the reader no less ignorant about the far North than he would be if he had never heard of Tacitus.

In the areas now called Denmark, Finland, Norway, and Sweden, the earliest evidences of human settlement go back ten thousand years or more. The indications are that most of the early settlements in Sweden were founded by newcomers who migrated there from Denmark. The meager evidence available suggests that agriculture and animal husbandry first appeared in the south of Sweden, which was part of the Danish domain until well past the middle of the seventeenth century. Fishing and hunting long remained important parts of the complicated business of living—no doubt more complicated even in those distant times than modern sophisticates are likely to assume.

About the early settlers of Finland almost nothing is known, but the forebears of the present-day inhabitants came from the lands south of the Gulf of Bothnia some two thousand years ago. Settling first in the southwest, they gradually pushed along the coasts and penetrated inland. The population remained small: it was probably no more than 400,000 as late as the sixteenth century and reached 1 million only after 1810. Even when the Finns emerged on the stage of history, in the eleventh and twelfth centuries, they had not yet developed the political organization we call a state; their basic organization was the clan, probably consisting of the descendants of common ancestors.

Finland's development prior to the eleventh century thus belongs in the domain of prehistory. So-called historical sources date back no further than 1100. Even the twelfth century offers only vague information of the events of the period. This lack is partly accounted for by the country's geographical location, for Finland was even farther off the beaten path than the other Scandinavian nations. For instance, the Church of Rome had become fairly generally accepted in Denmark while the people in Finland were still in the earliest stages of their conversion to the new faith. And it is of special interest that the earliest and sharpest outlines of Finland's meager historical record in the Middle Ages were etched by the Catholic Church and its servants. More important, however, is the fact that Scandinavia in general was a faraway frontier region; it was settled relatively late and became part of the European culture only centuries after the peoples and countries farther south or west.

Although human habitation has existed in Denmark for some twelve thousand years, the Danes, as a nation "with a history of their own," do not appear on the historical scene until about 800 A.D. It would probably be an oversimplification to say of the Danes—as of the Finns, the Norwegians, and the Swedes—that their real historical record begins with the introduction of Christianity. The arrival of the monk Ansgar in Denmark in the year 826, however, literally marked the beginning of an era in which Denmark's political and religious history was to correspond to the patterns of the western European nations. In its early phases, that history was far from tranquil: much of the twelfth century, for instance, was marked by a prolonged struggle between Crown and Church. A reconciliation was not effected until about 1170. Bloody dynastic rivalries also punctuated these early years which are largely hidden, in Denmark as well as in the rest of Scandinavia, in the darkness of unrecorded history.

The Viking Period (ca. 850-1050) is unique in the early history of the North. Much less is known about it than would be necessary for a full understanding, yet a great deal has been written about it. Karen Larsen, in her well-known A *History of Norway*, has correctly remarked that it is "the only epoch in the history of Norway before the nineteenth century to which much attention has been devoted by students outside of the North itself." The archaeological remains that form the main source of information about these centuries do not allow a very deep penetration into the essentials of the conditions or the society that produced the so-called Viking Age. Supplementary literary sources fall far short of explaining the unusual overseas enterprise and expansion that marked this period.

The Vikings, although not entirely unlettered, were far from that stage of political and general cultural development that leads to— perhaps requires—the keeping of records of events, plans, policies, taxes, laws, and so on. By the time the rudiments of such records and the beginnings of Scandinavian literary endeavor emerged in the thirteenth century, the memory of the details and personalities of the Viking Era had largely vanished. Modern students are therefore forced to rely almost wholly on the information that comes from the lands the Vikings raided and pillaged. This fact alone invites the conclusion that contemporary descriptions of the Vikings are possibly overly hostile. Many historians have exalted them as great heroes, incomparable seafarers, and examples of an upsurge of "national" energies; others have seen them as little more than successful pirates and plunderers unworthy of praise or adulation.

One factor frequently mentioned as a basic cause of the expansionist tendencies of the Vikings is the overpopulation of Scandinavia at that time. The explanation seems reasonable and helpful, but it is —at the very least—an oversimplification. No convincing evidence of overpopulation in Scandinavia has been advanced. Furthermore, societies that live primarily by fishing, hunting, and similar food-gathering techniques do not experience a sudden and marked growth in population. The alleged "population explosion" leading to the Viking expansion could have come about only as the result of a notable expansion of agriculture. There appears to be, however, no evidence of such an expansion during the period before, say, 800 A.D. Therefore, overpopulation must be rejected as a cause and the problem, for the time being, remains unsolved.

The Viking raids covered a wide area. Ireland, western Scotland,

and England felt their weight, especially after 800 A.D. The Vikings attacked Paris in 845; Normandy fell to them in the tenth century, and the German lands were devastated. The Orkney and Shetland Islands, Iceland, and Greenland testified to Viking successes in Atlantic waters. The mainland of North America was reached in the eleventh century by daring seafarers from Iceland and Norway, but the discovery led neither to permanent settlements nor to a general awareness of the continent later discovered by Columbus.

A large part of England fell into the hands of the Vikings. They would probably have penetrated farther had it not been for the decisive victory won by King Alfred the Great in 878 A.D. Under the agreement that followed Alfred's victory, the Danes retained control of the eastern coastal region known as Danelaw, where they established permanent settlements. Well over a century later, Canute the Great captured nearly the whole of England. By 1018 he had become king of England and Denmark—where his influence probably was very slight—and shortly thereafter king of Norway as well. "Danish" rule over England ended shortly after his death (1035), when the crown went again to an English king.

Swedish Vikings—many of whom also joined Danish and Norwegian chieftains in plundering and levying tribute in the west—also traveled, fought, conquered, and traded eastward. According to old chronicles, they "founded" the Russian state. Some pressed farther and served in the Eastern Empire in Constantinople. Evidences of Viking invasion and enterprise reveal they ultimately extended their forays to the Mediterranean as well.

The Norwegian overseas enterprises during the Viking Period differed in an important respect from those of their Scandinavian brethren: theirs alone resulted in lasting Northern settlements abroad, in which the prevailing language and culture remained basically those of the mother country. This was true of the Shetland Islands, the Faroes, the Orkneys, and especially Iceland. Emigration, appropriation of land, and settlement characterized the Norwegian aspect of the period and, in turn, left impressions on the homeland different from those observable in the other Viking lands.

It is not until the Middle Ages that anything like a continuing record of Scandinavian history begins to emerge. A Norwegian scholar has aptly remarked that Norway's Middle Ages began only with the "introduction of Christianity, during the early part of the eleventh century," and points out that the years 1030-1537 span the medieval period.[1] The same statement applies to Sweden and Finland as well, nor is Denmark an exception (although there the beginning date is earlier). But even the phrase *Middle Ages* represents, in this context, something of an oversimplification, for adequate sources for the history of the Scandinavian peoples do not date back further than the thirteenth century. It is this circumstance that led a well-known Swedish historian to remark that one of Sweden's kings, who died as late as 1470, was "one of the first notable medieval figures in Sweden whose personality can be fairly easily deduced from contemporary sources." [2]

When the mists that hide most of Scandinavia's past before 1300 begin to lift, Sweden and Finland are already part of the same realm, under a common king, and living under basically the same legal, religious, and political institutions. How this order of things, destined to last until the nineteenth century, had come about, is one of the many fascinating questions in Scandinavian history.

Until fairly recently, many historians were ready to offer explanations that seemed factually sound and logical. The explanations rested upon the conclusions of eighteenth-century historians, elaborated and seemingly confirmed by the writers in the nineteenth century. According to these sources, King Erik of Sweden, accompanied by the English-born Bishop Henry of Uppsala, undertook a crusade to Finland in 1157 for the purpose of baptizing the Finns. The success of the enterprise extended the dominion of Sweden and the Roman Catholic Church to Finland. Bishop Henry, who was killed shortly thereafter by a Finnish chieftain, became the national saint of Finland. The spring near Turku in southwest Finland, at which the mass baptism allegedly took place, became an "historical" site and—in recent decades—something of a tourist attraction.

Yet this account must be tossed on the heap of historical discards. It rests, literally, on historically valueless legends of saints compiled in Sweden toward the end of the thirteenth century, and on a Finnish folk poem that dates from about 1400. The Church of Rome is silent on the subject of the introduction of Christianity into Finland (although two papal bulls, one from 1172 and another from 1209, refer

---

[1] Dr. Martin Blinheim, in *The American Scandinavian Review* (December 1963), 355.

[2] Ingvar Anderson, *A History of Sweden*, translated by Carolyn Hannay (New York: Frederick A. Praeger, Inc., 1956), p. 93.

to that country). Nor is there any documentary record of how the land of the Finns gradually became a part of Sweden. We must, therefore, look elsewhere for the answer to this question.

A study of medieval graves has shown that Christian burial customs had become general in the older, settled parts of Finland at least a century before the alleged crusade. Christian beliefs and practices had thus existed in Finland long enough before the twelfth century to prepare the ground for the prominent position the Church had come to occupy by the early fourteenth century.

The legend of the crusade implies that Finland was brought, by force of arms, into a union with Sweden that was destined to last for centuries. This claim or explanation must also be discarded. First, it rests exclusively on the fanciful legend of the crusade and on the alleged conversion of the Finns at sword's point. No other evidence or record exists to support this thesis. Second, it runs counter to many aspects of the later political and social conditions in Finland that could have developed only in a free society equal to or identical with that which existed in Sweden.

There never was a Swedish "conquest" of Finland in the usual sense of the word. No historical record or tradition exists that describes or hints at events that destroyed the Finns' freedom, despoiled them of their lands, or bound them against their will to the status of a subject people. To contend the contrary is to disregard facts that define clearly enough, especially after 1300, the position of the Finns in the Swedish kingdom.

Finland became a part of Sweden centuries before Sweden's unification had proceeded far enough to destroy the province as the basic political unit, and while concepts of law and administrative organization still had little meaning outside the provinces that constituted the kingdom. The realm consisted of several "lands," of which Finland was one. Its status and rights were the same as those of the provinces in Sweden proper. While the monarchy remained elective—it became hereditary as late as 1544—the Finns participated in the election of kings. Finland was, and remained until 1808-1809, an integral part of the kingdom.

The development of this exceptional state of affairs has never been fully described because historical records are scarce. It seems clear, however, that the two peoples had been in contact with each other long before history began to record their fortunes; Swedes had settled, hunted, and traded in Finland for centuries. There probably were no great differences in the social development of the two peoples; sparsely populated Finland offered no tempting opportunities for economic exploitation which might have led to friction and violent clashes of interests; and neither country had a strong central government able to command adequate fighting forces. These and related circumstances no doubt account for one of the most remarkable phenomena in the North: the absence of conflict between Finns and Swedes during the long centuries that preceded the cession of Finland to Russia in 1809.

Toward the end of the medieval period, the Danes, the Finns, the Norwegians, and the Swedes were united under a common king. The union, usually called the Kalmar Union, was established in 1397 and ended in the 1520s when Sweden broke away. The Union was the handiwork of Queen Margaret of Denmark, unquestionably one of the most remarkable personages of Scandinavia.

Margaret (1352-1412) was the daughter of the king of Denmark and the wife of the king of Norway. In 1376, her father died, whereupon her six-year-old son became king of Denmark and Margaret was named regent. Her husband's death in 1380 brought her son, then ten years of age, to the throne, and Margaret was named regent of Norway as well. The son came of age in 1385, but he reigned for only two years. Upon his death in 1387, Margaret was chosen queen of Denmark (she was named regent of Norway in 1388). Making use of Norwegian claims to the Swedish throne and skillfully navigating the course of baronial conflicts and policies, she succeeded in becoming regent of Sweden in 1388. She brought forth a grandnephew of hers—Erik, born in 1382—as the candidate for the three thrones and succeeded in having him chosen king of the three countries in 1389-96. A dynastic union had thus been brought about. The three kingdoms it comprised were large, but their population probably did not exceed 1.5 million, over half of whom were Danes.

But although the three countries now had the same king, their governments and administration remained fully separate. Margaret tried to make the union complete. In 1397, she convened an assembly of notables from the North at Kalmar, a city in southeast Sweden. The purpose of the assembly was to draft an instrument providing for a closer union among the three countries. The so-called Kalmar Union, however, never developed into more than a dynastic arrangement. Its history during the fifteenth century repeatedly demonstrated the fact that the same baronial interests and political ambitions which had made the union possible also served to challenge and ultimately to destroy it. The Kalmar agreement rested on no popular mandate delivered by the representatives of the people at large; thus it was especially vulnerable to the changing purposes of the nobles and politicians in their quest for privilege and power.

Weak and unimportant as the Kalmar Union was, it has often been credited with having secured peace in Scandinavia for a relatively long period. This is, however, only partly true. After Margaret's death in 1412, the Danish-led Union imposed increasing tax and other burdens on the Norwegians, the Swedes, and the Finns. A substantial Swedish revolt against the Danes broke out in 1434—it led, incidentally, to the convocation of a general Swedish assembly in 1435, usually considered the beginning of the Swedish Riksdag—and the Norwegians revolted in 1436. Although the Union withstood these revolts, it almost fell apart in the late 1440s, and the following decades witnessed repeated crises: one of the outstanding Swedish leaders of the time, Karl Knutson, was elected king of Sweden, in defiance of the Danes, not less than three times (he was king in 1448-57, 1464-65, and 1467-70). But each time his claim to the throne was successfuly challenged. Sweden and Denmark were at war intermittently in the 1490s and again in 1501-23.

Neither Norway nor Finland occupied the center of the stage during the conflicts between the supporters of the Union and its opponents. Both, however, felt the consequences of the Danish leadership of the Union. Finland, as part of Sweden, broke away when Gustavus Vasa's successful revolt in 1521-23 led to the establishment of a national Swedish monarchy. Norway, on the other hand, remained affiliated with Denmark, until 1814. The results of the long union with Denmark were destined to have a lasting effect on Norway and its history, especially before the nineteenth century.

The revolt sparked by Gustavus Vasa was the direct result of a war launched by the Danes against the Swedes in 1517. Fortune favored the forces of Christian II, who had become king of Denmark in 1513. The Swedes laid down their arms in September 1521 and, after solemnly promising to pardon those who had fought against him, Christian was crowned in November. Less than two years later, he arbitrarily ordered the execution of over eighty leading Swedes who—with royal assurances of safety—had been invited to an assembly in the Stockholm Royal Castle. The "Stockholm Blood Bath" touched off the Swedish revolt and marked the beginning of the end of the Union itself.

## Sweden-Finland

The Swedish revolt, led by Gustavus Vasa, destroyed the Kalmar Union. Gustavus, who had been aided in his endeavors by the outbreak of civil war in Denmark, was elected king of Sweden in 1523, became hereditary monarch in 1544, and ruled until 1560. Danish hegemony in the North was thus replaced by a dynastic and political split that, by dividing the North in two, defined the main outward contours of Scandinavia until the early years of the nineteenth century. Two "national" monarchies had taken the place of the Kalmar Union: Sweden-Finland and Denmark-Norway. Each was destined to go its own way and to play different roles in the history of the North.

The decades of Gustavus Vasa's rule not only witnessed the establishment of Sweden's independence from Danish control but also saw the emergence of a national church both in Sweden and in Denmark. The Reformation produced major changes in both countries (including Finland, as a part of Sweden, and Norway, as a part of the Danish domain). The Reformation succeeded not because of a popular religious revival or protest against the Church of Rome; it was the direct result of the determination of the Crown to "nationalize" the Church and to lay hands upon its wealth. Devout churchmen who had come under Luther's influence also played important roles in the process. That the spoliation of the Church's property and the introduction of the Lutheran creed precipitated no widespread or prolonged protest among the people perhaps indicates the failure of Catholic precepts and practices to sink deep during the few centuries Scandinavia had been within Rome's fold. The change was accomplished with a minimum of friction, and the Northern lands have remained the most conspicuous Lutheran stronghold in Europe.

The two and a half centuries that separate the Reformation from the French Revolution and the Napoleonic Era witnessed many changes in Scandinavia. By 1600, Sweden-Finland had become a monarchy in which the king not only held the crown by hereditary right but also represented a national government centralized to a degree unknown before the stern and energetic rule of Gustavus Vasa. Gustavus has been called, with good reason, the founder of a new Sweden. He devoted much attention to agriculture and the development of trade and mining; and in many ways he governed his kingdom as if it had been a huge personal farm or business enterprise. (It was under his rule, incidentally, that Stockholm became the capital and the first permanent residence of the king.) During the fifty years that followed Gustavus' death in 1560, the reigns of his successors—his three sons—demonstrated over and over again that "war is the king's business." These years also witnessed the rise of a pretentious landed nobility which vied with the Crown for lands and influence. The beginnings of Sweden's Baltic empire were established when Estonia was secured between the 1560s and 1581.

When Gustavus Adolphus ascended the throne in 1611, his inheritance included three unfinished wars and a country in need of peace and administrative reform. An able soldier and administrator, he was endowed with qualities of mind and character that made him outstanding both as a man and as the leader of a nation. War absorbed most of his attention. In 1630, he entered the lists against the German imperial forces in what is known as the Thirty Years' War. By the time he was killed in battle—at Lutzen on November 6, 1632—he had successfully aided the Protestant cause and stemmed the Catholic tide (partly with the aid of subsidies from Catholic France, interested in defeating the Habsburgs). It was one of the ironies of history that his daughter and successor, Christina, laid down her crown in 1654, renounced the Lutheran creed, and became a Catholic.

Northern historians in general and Swedish historians in particular speak of the years 1611-1718 as the Age of Greatness. As the result of Gustavus Adolphus' successful policies and operations, ably carried forward after his death by his chancellor, Axel Oxenstierna, Sweden became one of the great powers of the day. By 1660, her prestige had been further enhanced by the conquest of the Danish provinces in what is today southern Sweden, and by further gains in the areas south of the Gulf of Finland. Although these and other developments placed severe and continuing strains upon the nation, its position in the Scandinavian and Baltic area was secure when Charles XII became king in 1697.

The reign of Charles XII turned out to be calamitous, bringing to an abrupt end the two decades of peace during which the kingdom had partly recovered from the effects of prolonged and costly wars. Fifteen years of age when he ascended the throne, war became his main interest and career until he was killed in the siege of an obscure Norwegian fortress in 1718. Charles has been highly praised by some historians and roundly condemned by others. He spent a dozen years abroad, fighting the Poles and the Russians in eastern Europe or as an exile in Turkey. Returning to Sweden in 1714, he resumed his fight against the Danes. His death led to a peace settlement in 1719-

21 which deprived Sweden of her possessions in the Baltic provinces and northern Germany. And the kingdom itself was subjected to its first severe territorial amputation: a large part of southeastern Finland was ceded to Russia in 1721.

This cession turned out to be merely the first of a series of territorial losses suffered by the kingdom. In 1741, long before the scars left by Charles XII's wars had healed, Sweden attacked Russia. The war ended in defeat and in another cession of territory in southeastern Finland. Another war against Russia, rashly begun in 1788, ended two years later without any change in Sweden's eastern frontier, but in 1808-1809 all of Finland was lost to the Russian Empire. It was small consolation to either Swede or Finn that the 1808-1809 war was not begun by Sweden but was caused by an agreement between Napoleon and Alexander I designed to force Sweden's participation in the continental blockade against England. Finland became a part of the Russian Empire, but as an autonomous nation with her own constitution, not as a subject province. (See Chapter Four.)

By 1809, Sweden had undergone significant political and constitutional changes as well. By the opening of the eighteenth century, the country had become, for all practical purposes, an absolute monarchy. The nobility, formerly a counterweight against the pretensions of the Crown, had been reduced in influence and had virtually become a class of civil servants and administrators. The Riksdag, which had emerged in the fifteenth century, had by the seventeenth century become representative of the Four Estates of the realm (nobles, clergy, burghers, and peasants), but it provided no check upon the powers of the king.

The end of the long and disastrous wars in 1721 ushered in a fifty-year period known in Swedish history, incongruously, as the Age of Freedom. During this half-century, the monarchy was reduced to complete impotence; all power was centered in the Royal Council and Riksdag—or, more particularly, in the hands of the party in control of the Riksdag. The liberty of neither the individual subject nor the nonprivileged classes in general was increased by the dominance of the legislature. Its rule has been aptly characterized as "unbridled political license and misrule" in which "the much-vaunted 'liberty' consisted of a freedom on the part of the members of the ascendant faction to line their own pockets, to the public detriment." [3]

The misrule of the Riksdag was ended by a coup engineered by Gustavus III in 1772. His reign ultimately led to a new royal abso-

[3] *Sweden—Ancient and Modern* (Stockholm, 1938), pp. 53, 54.

lutism, embodied especially in an "Act of Union" in 1789. The unlimited monarchy foisted upon the country by Gustavus III endured
until 1809. But because his foreign and domestic adventures created
a good deal of opposition, Gustavus himself was assassinated in
1792. Sweden thus entered the nineteenth century under the yoke of
royal absolutism.

### Denmark-Norway

The dissolution of the Kalmar Union caused a considerable reduction of Denmark's domination of the North. It did not, however, lead
to a recognition of the fact that Sweden's emergence as a national
monarchy had changed the power relationships in the Scandinavian
and Baltic area. Nor did it mean that Denmark had abandoned the
effort to recapture the leadership that had once been hers.

One of the immediate results of the Swedish revolt was the forced
abdication of King Christian II in 1522. His successor, Frederick I,
set the stage for an attack upon the position and property of the
Church which led to the introduction of Protestantism in Denmark.
The process was completed in 1536, less than a decade after Gustavus
Vasa had brought the Church in Sweden to heel. An assembly of the
Estates was convened in Copenhagen, in October 1536, to define the
new position of the Church. (The assembly was notable for the fact
that it was the last, for about three centuries, in which the peasants
would be represented.) The new state church professed the Lutheran
creed, based on the Augsburg Confession. Its supreme head was now
the king. Its property, and that of the bishops, as well as the tithes of
the devout were confiscated by the Crown. The holdings of the
Crown grew immensely until they represented over half the lands
of the country. Henceforth the clergy in Denmark and Norway were
to be civil servants, as they were in Sweden and Finland.

In Denmark, the growth of royal authority and the concentration
of power in the hands of the king set off a prolonged and complicated
reaction. The main opponents of the monarchy were the nobles; the
lower orders—the burghers and the peasants—did not become important in the political life of the nation until after the middle of the
nineteenth century. The nobles, on the other hand, appeared in
the picture at an early date. In 1282, for example, they had forced the
king to accept participation in government by a council of nobles, the
Council of the Danish Realm. The Council remained a part of the
monarchy's governmental apparatus until 1660 when all restrictions
on royal power came to an end.

One of the consequences of the political and religious developments of the 1530s was the loss by the burghers and the peasants of
whatever political influence they had had earlier. By the middle of
the seventeenth century, the general condition of the peasants—
about nine tenths of whom were leasehold farmers—had greatly de-
teriorated; a particular burden was the increase in labor they were
obligated to perform for the landlords. Meanwhile, the financial
position of the Crown was rendered stronger by the continued collection of dues that had been levied since 1425 on ships that passed
through Danish waters to and from the Baltic. The levy yielded increasing amounts over the years and contributed to the royal treasury
until 1857, when it was ended by international agreement. Under
these circumstances, there emerged no representative institutions
providing constitutionally guaranteed, regular burgher and peasant
participation in the conduct of public business. King and Council—
i.e., the leaders of the nobility—therefore provided for state and nation unless, as frequently happened, they were at loggerheads and vied
among themselves for controlling influence.

The position and prerogatives of the Danish nobility had evolved
in a manner that was, in some respects, unique. The nobility had
become something of a closed caste by about 1450, when it was composed of about 260-odd families. Because a nobleman, in order to
enjoy freedom from taxation and other privileges, had to prove that
his forebears had been tax-exempt for at least three generations, the
class had shrunk to some 3000 persons by 1650. But neither their
small numbers nor the envy and hate of the lower orders prevented
the nobles from asserting, whenever possible, their rights and privileges against king and commoners. Their position and pretensions
had much to do with the setting up of an exceptional type of royal
absolutism in 1660-65. (See Chapter Five.)

Denmark's determination to recover something of the position she
had enjoyed before the Swedish revolt led her to undertake a series
of wars with Sweden. During the long reign of Christian IV (1588-
1648), Denmark fought Sweden in 1611-13 and was persuaded to
intervene in the Thirty Years' War in 1626-29. The encounters resulted in defeats for Denmark. The end of still another war, in
1657-58, found Denmark forced to cede extensive areas to Sweden,
among them Skåne in the south (which gave Sweden her present
southern boundaries). The Danes tried to recover Skåne in still
another war, but had to accept the cession as permanent in 1660.

These military defeats provided the background for the revolutionary change in 1660 that ushered in the royal absolutism embodied in the King's Law of 1665. (See also Chapter Four.) Although all Danes were thenceforth considered to be on the same level before the absolute rule of the king, the new law did not eliminate social or economic distinctions, and the class structure remained as rigid as before. Indeed, the peasants were forced into an ever more insecure status in the eighteenth century. Between the 1730s and the 1780s, most male peasants between the ages of fourteen and thirty-six were bound, virtually as serfs, to the estates on which they were born. These rights of landowners over their tenants were later extended.

The harsh exactions of the landowners were temporarily eased in the 1770s but no real relief came until a significant reform was carried out between 1784 and 1788, when serfdom was abolished. The peasant was now free to acquire and farm his own plot of land. The ultimate aim of the reform was to establish freehold ownership of the land; in introducing this measure, Denmark became a pioneer in this area of agricultural reform.

The Napoleonic Wars had a disastrous effect upon Denmark. She was forced into the conflict by Britain's determination to prevent the Danish fleet from being taken and used by Napoleon. The English therefore bombarded Copenhagen in July 1807, sank part of the Danish fleet, and sailed the rest to England. In retaliation, Denmark joined with Napoleon in the seven hard years that followed. At the end of the war, the victorious British and their allies hammered out a peace settlement that meant, among other things, serious losses for Denmark—outstanding among which was the cession of Norway to Sweden.

Half a century after the loss of Norway, Denmark was forced to accept another peace settlement that further reduced her territory. Two largely German duchies, Schleswig and Holstein, had been connected with the Danish Crown since the Middle Ages and had caused periodic friction and difficulty between Germany and Denmark over the years. In 1848, they had revolted against Danish attempts to incorporate them as integral parts of the realm. The two-year war that followed, which provoked armed intervention by Prussia on the side of the duchies, resulted in a Danish victory. But the problem was not permanently solved, and in 1864, after another war with Germany and Austria, Denmark was forced to relinquish the disputed provinces. The loss of the duchies was partly made up in 1920, when the northern part of Schleswig was incorporated in Denmark after a plebiscite in which the Danish elements overwhelmingly voted for union with the mother country. Finland's and Norway's new position and political affiliation lasted, without basic change, for about a century. The Swedish-Norwegian union, after a great deal of friction, was peacefully severed in 1905, when Norway became a fully sovereign nation. Finland's union with Russia was ended in 1917-18, when World War I and the Russian Revolution gave the Finns an opportunity to become fully independent.

# THREE

# SCANDINAVIA AND WORLD WAR I

## On the Eve of War

The foreign policies and relations of the Scandinavian nations before 1914 had long been such as to place them outside the mainstream of Big-Power agreements or alliances; they were designed to maintain peace and neutrality and to avoid undertakings likely to create friction or endanger cordial relations with other states. The Scandinavian nations had no territorial ambitions; neither did they suffer from minority problems likely to disturb their relations with other nations. They had no colonial ambitions, and they pursued peaceful commercial undertakings with the outside world, requiring no preferential treatment anywhere. They regarded war as only a remote possibility, perhaps because they had no clear idea of the difficulties involved in keeping out of it.

Immediately after the outbreak of World War I, each of the Scandinavian nations (except Finland, which was not yet independent) issued a declaration of neutrality—the declarations were issued separately but were nearly identical in wording—and managed, by luck and pluck, to escape involvement. It was not fully understood at the time, however, that their success in avoiding involvement had depended not only on their resolve to remain neutral but also on the fact that the warring nations did not feel it necessary to violate them. Only after World War II did it become clear that neutrality is honored only if and when it creates no serious problems for the vital interests of the belligerent nations.

The Scandinavian countries were, needless to say, wholly unprepared for the conditions created by war. The fear that food supplies were low and that foreign trade would quickly cease and leave the people exposed to starvation caused a run on stores: in some cities the price of rye bread increased by 30 per cent within a week after the outbreak of hostilities; that of flour, by over 300 per cent. Runs on the banks also occurred; the desire to hoard gold and silver was as great as that to hoard food. The panic subsided quickly, however, and the governments proceeded to deal with the three basic problems caused by the war: (1) the procurement of essential food supplies; (2) the maintenance of industry, farming, and the national economies in general on an even keel, despite shortages of raw materials, dislocations of normal trade connections, and loss of foreign markets; and (3) the safeguarding of neutrality by avoiding actions or commitments that might lead to involvement in the conflict.

In dealing with these and related problems, the governments of Scandinavia illustrated, on a smaller scale, the experiences of the great and small powers directly involved in the war. The years 1914-18 witnessed an enormous expansion of the business of government. New departments, agencies, and offices were established and old ones were greatly expanded. Government aims were to conserve and safeguard food supplies and prevent runaway inflation by establishing price ceilings and other controls; to regulate the export of certain commodities or to prohibit the import of others; to secure the supply of certain basic essentials, such as coal and grain; and to save grain and potatoes, for example, by forbidding the production and even the sale of intoxicating beverages. In Norway, where shipping was most vital to the country's economy, compulsory insurance of ships was introduced, with the government assuming a large part of the costs. These were only some of the war-imposed activities that resulted in the great expansion of government and in the enlargement of its function at national and local levels. They also resulted in growing expenses, larger budgets, heavier taxation, and great increases in the national debts.

When World War I began, the situations of Denmark, Finland, Norway, and Sweden differed in several respects. Norway had become fully sovereign only nine years earlier—in 1905, when the union with Sweden was dissolved. The country commemorated in May 1914 the centenary of its constitution and the progress and achievements of the nation during the century that had passed since its adoption. A sense of security and a spirit of optimism characterized the nation through the spring and early summer of the fateful year 1914.

Denmark had emerged from an important constitutional struggle in 1901, when the Moderate Liberal party—which had held the majority of seats in the lower chamber ever since 1872—succeeded in overcoming conservative opposition and establishing a government. The importance of domestic concerns in Denmark was underlined by the developments that led, in 1915, to liberal changes in the constitution—among them, the establishment of the predominance of the popularly elected lower house of the national legislature, the limitation of the electoral privileges of the upper house, and the extension of the right to vote to women and certain other disenfranchised groups.

Sweden, too, was occupied with domestic concerns in 1914. The bitter disappointment felt in many quarters over the dissolution of the union with Norway had largely disappeared. Both countries had joined Denmark in issuing neutrality rules in 1912. Reform of the franchise—only some 10 per cent of the people had the right to vote at the turn of the century—was put through in 1907, doubling the size of the electorate, and the ground was being prepared for the political emancipation of the women in 1918. Attempts by liberal and labor elements to introduce responsible, parliamentary government dominated the political scene; although cabinet responsibility did not become a part of the Swedish constitutional system until 1917, prevailing discussions and debates pointed the direction, even before 1914, in which Swedish progressive endeavors were to proceed. Social Democratic labor was still far from strong enough to capture and hold the reins of power, but it was soon to emerge as one of the main determinants of the nation's political life.

The period 1909-14 also witnessed the rise of two problems of special Swedish national interest and concern. One involved disputes between workers and employers. Strikes, lockouts, clashes between strikers and strikebreakers, and other conflicts had become common. The general strike called by labor in August 1909—some 300,000 workers were involved—failed, and the national trade union organization, the L.O. (*Landsorganisationen*) suffered a serious defeat. Meanwhile, significant beginnings were made in the field of social legislation. A more sensational and disturbing question, that of national defense, held the center of the stage late in 1913 and early in 1914. Social Democrats and Liberals in particular favored economies in defense outlay. The 1911 election program of the Liberals—whose leader, Premier K. Staaf, held office at the time—called for lowered defense expenditures. Staaf proceeded to effect economies and, in doing so, precipitated a political conflict of unusual intensity. It culminated in a demonstration in Stockholm in February 1914 of some 30,000 farmers who waited upon the king and demanded a speedy strengthening of both the army and the navy. The king openly supported the farmers' demands, and was thereupon charged by the cabinet with having indulged in unconstitutional action. The clash between Crown and cabinet resulted in the resignation of the government. The defense problem was still the source of serious debate and controversy when the outbreak of the war in the summer of 1914 changed the situation and forced the nation to face the new and insistent problems precipitated by the European turmoil. Internal divisions were abruptly ended, and Sweden stood united to maintain its neutrality in the midst of a worldwide conflagration.

Finland's situation on the eve of the war was markedly different from that of her sister nations of the North. Still part of the Russian Empire, Finland's position had become increasingly precarious during the preceding fifteen years. Her separate constitution and laws— solemnly recognized by Alexander I in 1809 and by all his successors down to Nicholas II, who became Tsar in 1894—had been repeatedly violated since 1890 and her autonomous status undermined. Under the pressure of the Russian Revolution of 1905, however, Nicholas II granted important constitutional reforms in Russia and rescinded the illegal measures that had destroyed much of Finland's self-rule during the preceding half-dozen years. But by 1908 a new policy of lawlessness and Russification was in full swing, and by 1914 it seemed that Finland's constitution, laws, and autonomous institutions were but chaff in the cold winds that once again blew from St. Petersburg. While the country at large stubbornly resisted Russification, a handful of patriots was secretly planning to end the threats to Finnish autonomy and to prepare Finland for emergence as a free nation.

### The Declarations of Neutrality

The declarations of neutrality issued by Denmark, Norway, and Sweden marked the beginning of the wartime cooperation of the three nations. The war was less than a week old when Sweden and Norway agreed, on August 8th, that they would under no circumstances permit the war in Europe to precipitate any hostile acts between the two countries. The agreement, which was also accepted by Denmark, established—for all practical purposes—a neutral entente of the North. Furthermore, in carrying forward their respective augmented defense efforts, Norway and Sweden could ignore their land frontiers and concentrate on coastal and naval defenses. Common dangers and interests thus broadened the area of accord among the three Scandinavian countries.

The neutrality policy of the Scandinavians was identical, in all basic respects, with the policy followed and defended by the United

States until early 1917. The Scandinavians and the Americans maintained that except in the case of contraband goods—clearly defined by international law and agreements going back to 1856—neutrals had a right to trade wherever and with whomever they would. The rights of the neutrals were violated from the first days of the war by the British, although the later German submarine campaign more than matched the British in this regard. Beginning late in August 1914, contraband lists and blockade rules were arbitrarily revised to fit British and general Entente needs. Germany likewise proceeded to violate international law by extending search and seizure of neutral ships and cargoes. These developments endangered the economies of the Scandinavians, in which foreign trade was a most vital factor. Faced with these growing dangers, the three governments issued a joint protest against the violation of their rights. The first protest, contained in a note of November 12, 1914, led to some temporary improvement in the situation, but as the war continued the belligerents paid less and less attention to pre-1914 proprieties and rules of warfare. Meanwhile, the expanded cooperation among the Northern countries was dramatized by the meeting of the three monarchs in Malmö in 1914, and in Christiania (now Oslo) in November 1917. The Malmö meeting, convened on Sweden's initiative, offered a conspicuous opportunity for emphatic demonstrations of Swedish-Norwegian amity. It went a long way toward effacing the memory of the friction caused by the 1814-1905 union and its dissolution less than a decade earlier.

Norway was in some respects in a more exposed position than her neighbors. This became especially clear in the autumn of 1915, when German trawlers and other ships entered Norway's coastal waters to buy fish directly from Norwegian fishermen. (These purchases caused a great increase in fish prices in the Norwegian domestic market and, thereby, dissatisfaction among the consumers.) The British threatened to retaliate by prohibiting the export of coal and oil to Norway. Such a prohibition, if put into effect, would have had disastrous consequences for Norway. The dilemma was resolved in a compromise arrangement, formalized by the Anglo-Norwegian Fish Agreement of August 5, 1916. Under this arrangement, Britain agreed to buy Norwegian fish in the open market at maximum prices fixed for the duration of the war—a precursor of the preclusive buying tactic, widely used during World War II—thereby depriving the Germans of the chance to replenish their food supplies. Norway was left with the right to uncontrolled exports of fish amounting to 15 per cent of the total catch. The agreement turned out to be anything but an unmixed blessing, for it ultimately contributed to inflationary price rises in Norway and also led Germany to take retaliatory action by sinking a number of Norwegian ships.

More serious difficulties appeared later, especially after the Germans began their unrestricted submarine campaign in February 1917. Norwegian losses in ships and sailors mounted so quickly that Norway entered into an agreement with Britain under which Britain was to take over and use Norwegian shipping during the war. The arrangement limited Norwegian losses, but did not end them. By the time the war ended, Norway had lost some 1.18 million tons (or nearly half) of her shipping, and about 2000 men. (Denmark's losses, incidentally, came to 243,700 tons of shipping and 670 men; Sweden's, to 201,400 tons and 1150 men.)

The loss of ships, sailors, and cargoes was only part of the burden imposed on Norway by the war. As the war progressed, some sectors of the country's industry slowed down or ground to a standstill because of the shortage of raw material and fuel and the dislocation of markets. Farming suffered because of lack of feeds and fertilizers. Because of the nation's dependence upon imports for a substantial part of its food, the contraction or disappearance of imports meant a lowered living standard and, in some cases, outright distress. Toward the end of the war, Norway's economy had assumed, to a large extent, the features of a planned war economy: rationing of a lengthening list of foods, price controls, regulations intended to ease shortages and adjust imports and exports as far as possible to the requirements of the hour. As one historian has put it, Norway experienced "practically all the effects of the war—except the devastations, of course— which the belligerent countries suffered." [1]

Sweden's experiences during the war paralleled, in the main, those of Norway. Sweden's propinquity to Russia appeared at first to present special problems for her neutrality, but it became clear before long that the difficulties involved in maintaining neutrality originated more in British and German practices than in Russian actions. Sweden was dependent upon imports for a substantial part of her essential foodstuffs. In the years before 1914, nearly one fifth of the rye, almost half of the wheat and somewhat less than one third of the cereals used in Sweden came from abroad. Feeds, fertilizers, and such industrial raw materials as coal, cotton, oil, lubricants, rubber, metals, and

[1] Karen Larsen, A History of Norway (Princeton, N.J.: Princeton University Press, 1948), p. 511.

machinery were indispensable for the normal functioning of the nation's economy, as was the sale abroad of wood products, paper, pulp, iron ore, and the products of the Swedish industries.

Sweden's neutrality policy attempted, understandably, to keep the country out of the war and to safeguard its economy by taking full advantage of the rights of neutrals as defined by international law and custom before 1914. But Sweden's "neutral rights," like Norway's, turned out to depend on the caprices of the belligerents who attempted to limit and control her exports and imports in accordance with their own interests. Economic necessity ultimately resulted in the establishment of state control over a large part of foreign trade. It also led to increased trade with Germany, especially in the early part of the war—vitally important coal, for example, could be most easily obtained from Germany, in exchange for Swedish iron ore and other products—while imports from Britain sharply declined because of shipping difficulties. Inflation, rising prices, sharp increases in the cost of living, rationing of many foods, and regulation of many commodities gradually appeared, along with speculation and profiteering, and became even more pronounced after the Germans began their campaign of unrestricted submarine warfare in 1917.

An indication of Sweden's wartime trials and tribulations is provided by the fact that per capita grain consumption in the nation had decreased, by 1917-18, to approximately half what it had been in 1913. In the spring and early summer of 1917, food riots broke out in several localities, caused in part by a serious potato shortage. The crop failure of 1917 added to the difficulties. The food situation was somewhat improved as the result of an agreement with Britain in March 1918—supplemented by agreements later—which provided for the importation of a wide variety of essential foods under guarantees that none would be exported to Germany. Sweden paid for the concession by leasing about half of her merchant shipping—some 400,000 tons—to Britain, and by agreeing to limit her exports to Germany. The end of the war brought a welcome end to the suffering and humiliations imposed on the country by a conflict for which she was in no sense responsible.

Denmark's neutrality involved particular problems from the very first days of the war. When Austria-Hungary declared war on Serbia —on July 28th, a week before the Big Powers became involved— Denmark was warned by Germany that any Danish military preparations would lead to German reprisals. Assurances of "benevolent neutrality" were demanded and given two days later. On August 5th, despite the Danish declaration of neutrality, Germany demanded to know—the demand was close to an ultimatum—if Denmark intended to mine the nine-mile-wide Storebelt separating Zealand (on which Copenhagen is located) from Fyn. It seemed clear that a negative answer would lead Germany to mine the sound herself. Denmark therefore undertook the mining, in order to avoid more serious consequences resulting from her proximity to Germany. Britain, informed of Denmark's decision, offered no protest. This incident was only one illustration of the seeming conviction in Berlin that the Danes had not yet forgotten their defeat of 1864, which had resulted in the loss of Schleswig-Holstein, and could therefore be counted on to assume an anti-German posture in due time. Denmark, of course, harbored no such inclinations and was resolved to remain strictly neutral.

To follow a strictly neutral policy meant to proceed along the same difficult path marked out for Norway and Sweden. In some respects, however, Denmark was in a relatively favorable position. Britain and the Entente in general had no easy way of cutting off Danish-German commercial exchange because most of it was carried on across land frontiers safe from British supervision or control. On the other hand, Germany controlled the eastern and southeastern reaches of the North Sea and, therefore, much of the vital Danish export-import trade dependent on North Sea routes. Denmark's situation was considerably eased in October 1914, when Britain agreed to allow Denmark to import certain important commodities on condition that they would be used in Denmark and not be exported to Germany. Beginning in May and June 1915, Denmark was allowed to import contraband goods under the same provisions.

Denmark's merchant shipping did not escape the paralyzing effects of the war. On February 4, 1915, Germany declared that a "danger zone" around Britain had been established and could be entered by neutral ships only at their own peril. The situation was complicated further when Britain retaliated by decreeing that all ships carrying goods to Germany must put in at British ports, no matter what their cargo. Although the decree was modified later, it meant an annoying and serious limitation of the Danes' freedom of action. In January 1917, Denmark concluded an agreement with Britain which assured speedier clearing of Danish ships through British waters and provided for Danish monthly coal imports of 100,000 tons per month in return for turning over 100,000 tons of Danish shipping to Britain. Later, all British exports to Denmark, except coal, were stopped because Britain believed the Danes were sending important provisions to

Germany. Britain's decision merely increased Denmark's commercial exchange with the hard-pressed Central Powers and with Sweden and Norway. Large quantities of Danish grain were exchanged for Norwegian chemicals sorely needed in Denmark, and for Swedish lumber, ore, and other essentials. The Danish government also found it necessary to establish control over a variety of foodstuffs, and over the collection and distribution of most of the country's agricultural production, which had been substantially reduced since 1914.

### Finland: Independence and Revolt

Finland's position and experiences during the war years were more dramatic than those of her neighbors. While Norway, Sweden, and Denmark strove, as independent states, to maintain their neutrality, the war years at first exposed Finland to new dangers of Russification and ultimately created conditions that enabled the Finns to declare their independence and to take their place in the ranks of free nations.

During the half-dozen years before 1914, Finland had been subjected to increasing Russian violations of her autonomy and constitution. Shortly after the war began, plans for saving the country from the disaster that had threatened during the preceding several years were drafted by ambitious independence men. From November 1914 to March 1915, efforts were made to bring about British and American intercession on Finland's behalf. In the United States, for example, Presidents Nicholas Murray Butler of Columbia, Arthur T. Hadley of Yale, and A. Lawrence Lowell of Harvard, as well as ex-President Howard Taft, were approached and agreed to use their influence to obtain guarantees of Finland's autonomy in the event that the United States were to participate in the peace settlement. In Britain, these and similar efforts understandably evoked no active response.

The Finns also attempted, late in 1914, to obtain Swedish aid in preparing the country for revolt and independence if and when the time for bold action should come. Rebuffed in Sweden, they turned to Germany. The German High Command, seeing in the Finns' determination to break away from Russia a potential chance to weaken the Russian war effort, ultimately provided military training for some 2000 young Finns who were willing to risk their future on the chance that the world war would offer opportunities to strike a blow for their country's freedom.

Instead, the war provided additional opportunities for arbitrary

Russian rule. By 1917 it seemed that Finland would soon be reduced to the status of a subject province ruled directly from the capital of the Tsars. But the Russian Revolution in March changed the situation almost overnight. The collapse of the autocratic regime gave Finland a chance to free itself from the oppressor.

Within two weeks after the overthrow of the Tsarist government, the Russian Provisional government, headed by Lvov, issued a manifesto that canceled the Russification ordinances and decrees that had passed since 1898. Finland's self-rule was again recognized as resting on and deriving from Finnish law. The Finnish legislature, elected in 1916, met on April 4, 1917.

An unusual electoral situation in 1916 had resulted, in the Social Democrats' winning 103 out of the 200 seats in the Finnish Parliament. The legislature that met on April 4th, and later determined the composition of the government, thus had a solid Socialist majority. The cabinet it formed was a coalition in which the Social Democrats had the deciding vote.

The Socialist-led cabinet failed to carry the national cause to victory. In July 1917 it sponsored and succeeded in passing a law which provided that the rights and prerogatives previously belonging to the Tsar were henceforth to be exercised by the Finnish legislature. It also specified, incongruously, that foreign affairs and questions relating to military matters or administration would still be subject to Russian decision. The so-called "power law" thus left vital areas of national concern in the hands of Russia. When the government, equally incongruously, decided not to submit the law to the Provisional Government in Petrograd for promulgation, the Provisional Government dissolved the Finnish legislature and called for new elections. The elections, held in early October, resulted in ninety-two seats for the Socialists and 108 seats for the non-Socialist parties.

The non-Socialist government formed after the new legislature convened introduced a declaration of independence, which was accepted by the parliament on December 6th. Independence declared, however, was not independence achieved. In the fall of 1918, radical, revolutionary elements captured the leadership of the Social Democratic party and of leading labor unions and, encouraged by the Bolshevik Revolution in Russia in November, they proceeded to prepare a revolution in Finland. The Soviet government, headed by Lenin, supported their efforts, despite the fact that the Bolshevik government had been the first to recognize Finland's independence (December 31, 1917). The Finnish Reds raised the banner of revolt on January 28, 1918, but they were defeated. The victory of the legal government over the Red uprising meant victory in a war that was a struggle for independence as well as a civil conflict, and it enabled Finland to emerge as a fully sovereign nation. Peace with the Soviet government was formally concluded by a treaty negotiated at Dorpat, Estonia, and signed on October 14, 1920.

---

FOUR

CONSTITUTIONS, PARLIAMENTS,

RESPONSIBLE GOVERNMENT

---

The democratic institutions of the Scandinavian nations and their concept of liberty under law set these countries apart from much of the rest of Europe. They have given continuing evidence since World War I, and particularly since 1945, of their capacity to use the instrumentalities of democratic representative government in meeting the changing needs of society. In doing so, Denmark, Finland, Norway, and Sweden offer fascinating evidence of the importance of tradition and experience in preparing a nation to meet the tests that face modern democracies. They demonstrate that democratic traditions are the real determinants of success or failure in the difficult art of self-government, and that liberty not earned by long submission to gradual and strenuous schooling in self-government is likely to remain an elusive goal rather than an accomplishment on which a nation can build.

The mere passage of time has not, of course, been the deciding factor in bringing the Scandinavians to their present maturity as democracies. In Sweden and Finland, the unbroken tradition of representative institutions spans five centuries, for the beginnings of the Swedish parliament can be dated from about 1435. In Norway, the first representative institution appeared as recently as 1814, while the Danish legislative assembly can be traced, strictly speaking, only from 1849. Thus the all-important right to representation emerged in Scandinavia at widely different times. It would be misleading, however, to conclude that a centuries-old parliament provides a more solid basis for modern democracy than one of more recent vintage. The Swedish parliament, for example, did not become important until the eighteenth century, and although it wrought mightily for a half-century (1718-72) in challenging and restricting royal power, it did not become the champion of popular rights until well over a century later. Without minimizing the significance of prenineteenth-century experience, it is safe to say that it was only in the nineteenth century that the political emancipation of the common man really began. The progress recorded at the turn of the twentieth century was far from impressive, but by the early 1920s seemingly permanent victories were registered. And the process had been completed in a surprisingly peaceful manner.

The triumph of political democracy in Scandinavia involved three main changes or reforms: the establishment or reorganization of national legislatures; the revision of suffrage laws; and the introduction of responsible or parliamentary forms of government. In some instances the changes were gradual and rooted in practices extending over a long span of years; in others they appeared almost overnight. Constitutional provisions, the mandates of precedent, and legislative enactments were part of the process. The end result was a largely uniform set of rules, prescriptions, and procedures on which the modern democracy of the four nations rests today.

## Norway

Norway was the first of the Scandinavian nations to adopt a modern constitution and a representative national assembly. Both were consequences of events set in motion by the politics of the Napoleonic Era. By 1807, the Corsican had subdued most of Europe, and it was his expectation that Britain, his sole remaining opponent, could be defeated if her economy were paralyzed. But the strict commercial blockade he established had two wide gaps: Denmark-Norway, and Sweden. To coerce both into observing the blockade became one of Napoleon's objectives. The British decided to forestall Napoleon by demanding that the Danish-Norwegian fleet be turned over to them for the duration of the war. When the Danish government refused, the British bombarded Copenhagen (in 1807), seized the fleet (the famous "Copenhagening" of the Danish fleet), and sailed it to Britain. This high-handed action led to a Danish alliance with Napoleon and outright war between Britain and Denmark.

These developments had ruinous consequences for Norway's economy and ultimately caused the dissolution of her union with Denmark—a union established in 1380. After Napoleon had been defeated at Leipzig in October 1813, Sweden—led by Bernadotte, one of the marshals of Napoleon's armies—successfully invaded Denmark. The brief war was concluded by the Treaty of Kiel (January 14, 1814), which provided for the cession of Norway to the king of Sweden. The Norwegians, who had had no voice in a decision that was radically to change their status and future history, were thus brought into an affiliation with Sweden that only a few of them welcomed and most would have preferred to avoid. Instead of meekly accepting the verdict of the treaty, the Norwegians ventured on a course intended to carry them to complete independence. On April 11, 1814, 112 representatives of the nation met at Eidsvoll, there to draft a constitution for a sovereign Norway.

The labors of the Eidsvoll Constituent Assembly were completed on May 17th, when the new constitution was signed and proclaimed as the fundamental law of the land. On the same day, the Assembly elected as king of Norway Christian Frederick, cousin of the reigning monarch of Denmark. The election was rendered meaningless by the determination of Britain, Russia, Austria, and Prussia to enforce the Treaty of Kiel. Norwegian resistance to this plan led to war between Norway and Sweden. A brief struggle, it began on July 29th and was ended by an armistice on August 14th. On October 10th the parliament received Christian Frederick's abdication, and on the 20th it voted for union with Sweden under a common monarch. On November 4th the legislature formally chose Karl XIII of Sweden to be king of Norway. Heir apparent to the throne of Sweden, Karl Johan (Bernadotte) took an oath on November 9th to uphold Norway's constitution. The process of bringing the kingdom of Norway into the union with Sweden was thus completed. Norway, now a constitutional monarchy enjoying the right to manage and control its own internal affairs, had ceased to be a part of the Danish political system.

The Eidsvoll Constitution has been called the last of the liberal European constitutions that grew out of the Revolutionary Era. It was, needless to say, a product of eighteenth-century thought adapted to the needs of a small nation. The principles it set forth and the governmental agencies and instrumentalities it delineated made it, at the time, the most progressive fundamental law in Scandinavia, if not in Europe. Basic human rights were guaranteed in terms not unlike those of the first ten amendments to the Constitution of the United States. The legislative assembly, the Storting, it provided for was unique in its day. A measure of the success of the Eidsvoll Constitution is the fact that the Storting proved itself to be an exceptionally viable institution destined ultimately to become the supreme authority in the land.

Although it is a unicameral body in that no distinction is made among candidates at election time, the legislature—once convened—selects one third of its membership to constitute the Lagting while the remaining two thirds form the Odelsting. The system represents a compromise arrangement, as it were; it is neither a fully bicameral nor fully unicameral legislature, and much of the legislative function is left in the hands of the full Storting. The size of the Storting originally varied according to the number of people entitled to vote. The number of seats had grown to 117 by 1859, when a constitutional change reduced it to 111. The last constitutional amendment defining the size of the legislature came in 1919, when the number of representatives was fixed at 150. Both the Lagting and the Odelsting deal with all laws. The Storting constitutes a plenary session in which budgets and other matters of major import, as well as bills on which the Lagting and the Odelsting cannot agree, are considered.

Liberal and forward-looking as the Eidsvoll Constitution was in many ways, its suffrage provisions were in keeping with the general spirit of the times. For a long time after 1814, the electorate was limited to about 7 per cent of the adult population. It was not until 1898, after decades of agitation, that Norway became the first of the Scandinavian nations to introduce unrestricted male suffrage. Women, however, did not get equal voting rights until 1913. The voting age, originally fixed at twenty-four years, was lowered to twenty-one years in 1946.

### Finland

The cession of Finland to Russia in 1809 did not end the constitutional development begun while the country was an integral part of Sweden and its inhabitants the political equals of the Swedes. Although the union with Russia inevitably brought about deviations from pre-1809 conditions, the meaningful constitutional essentials remained intact. These furnished the basis for the nation's further constitutional and political evolution and made possible the development, after the 1860s, of a more effective legislative assembly and an orderly liberalization of the franchise. Both the national legislature and the franchise had become, by 1906, as democratic as any in Europe.

The constitutional framework in which Finland assumed her autonomous status within the Russian Empire was far from liberal. It embodied the constitutional changes that, in 1772 and 1789, had set up a strong royal power in Sweden and greatly reduced the powers of the legislative branch. But, although heavily weighted in favor of the monarchy, the constitution required the participation and consent of the legislature for the enactment of new laws, the imposition of taxes, and the amendment of the constitution itself. No less important was the fact that the arrangements in 1809 that created Finland as a self-governing state involved the grafting of no new, constitutionally incongruous or repellent elements onto traditional principles and practices. Thus what might well be called "the constitution of 1809," although far from adequate to the changing needs that had emerged before the mid-nineteenth century, represented a most important link with the past. It was also of immense value as a protection against the arbitrariness of the Tsar-Grand Duke, whose autocratic rule in Russia was limited by no constitutional restraints. The success of the Finns in persuading the Tsars to carry on, on the whole, as constitutional monarchs in Finland for the better part of a century—long before Russia herself obtained even the modest beginnings of a constitutional government—is one of the most fascinating aspects of Finland's history after 1809.

The Finns not only succeeded in retaining the laws and liberties that had been theirs for generations before 1809, but by the close of the nineteenth century they had managed greatly to enlarge the role and functions of the national legislature. The legislature was, after 1809, the Finnish equivalent of the Swedish Riksdag, as that assembly had been defined in 1772 and 1789: its powers were limited, and the convocation and the duration of its sessions depended upon the decision of the monarch. After 1809, the Finnish Diet was not convoked until 1863. Finland's legislative structure therefore remained virtually unchanged for over half a century. During the period before 1863, old laws and decrees, and ordinances based upon them, sufficed to meet the needs of the day without violations of the constitution. By the early 1860s, however, economic, and political problems had emerged that required the reactivation of the Diet. Alexander II was persuaded to summon the legislature to meet on September 18, 1863. The date marks the beginning of a new and significant chapter in the general history of Finland and especially in the history of its representative institutions.

The Diet of 1863 was a replica of the Swedish Riksdag of 1808. It was composed of four chambers or Estates: the nobles, the clergy, the burghers, and the peasants. At the 1809 Diet, the membership of the Estates was small, because of the war (seventy nobles, eight clergy, nineteen burghers, and thirty peasants, or a total of 127). The 1863 legislature was larger: 161 nobles, thirty-one clergy, thirty-seven burghers, and forty-six peasants. (Because each Estate had only one vote in the plenary sessions of the Diet, the difference in the size of each was a matter of no real moment.) The assembly was—and remained for several years after 1863—primarily a consultative body that could petition, but not by itself enact laws. Its area of function, however, was gradually enlarged. The Diet enacted a new Diet Law in 1867, promulgated in 1869, that provided for Diet sessions at least at five-year intervals—shortly changed to three-year intervals—and simplified rules of procedure as well. By the 1880s, it had won the right to initiate legislation in most matters. The Finnish Diet had thus proceeded substantially beyond the limits of competence of the Swedish Riksdag before 1809.

The four-Estate Diet and the restricted suffrage laws in force in the 1860s and for many years thereafter came to be seen as anachronisms by liberal and progressive elements. By 1906, however, the legislature had shown itself, despite its cumbersome organization and limited powers, capable of enacting laws required by a changing and increasingly industrialized society, and of defining in many respects and more sharply the autonomous position of the country as a part of the Russian Empire. A separate Finnish currency was introduced in 1865; industry, trade, and economic life in general were gradually freed from the restraints of guild and state; local administration was improved; a system of state-controlled and state-directed public schools was established in 1866; the relations of state and church were redefined in a more progressive spirit; and the language rights of the Finnish majority were asserted and carried forward in a manner that established, in 1902, the complete equality (as official languages) of Finnish and Swedish.

The piecemeal reforms from the 1860s to the end of the nineteenth century were only preliminaries to the democratic breakthrough of 1906. The stage for the 1906 reforms was set by the defeat of Russia in the 1904-1905 war with Japan. During the war, Finnish sympathies were overwhelmingly on the side of the Japanese, although open expressions were prevented by political prudence and common sense. The Russian defeat in the war precipitated a revolutionary movement, the results of which were felt in Finland as well. It led to concessions by the Russian government that included the repeal of a series of measures that had violated Finland's constitution and laws during the preceding half-dozen years. The new situation also resulted in the presentation of a bill providing for a new and radical reform of the Diet. The measure, accepted by the Diet and promulgated on July 20, 1906, revolutionized the national legislature. The antiquated four-Estate assembly was voted out of existence by the "unreconstructed"

Diet itself, and replaced by a unicameral parliament of 200 members. No less important was the thorough democratization of the franchise. All adult men and women were given the right to vote, without any property qualifications. The right to vote meant the right to be chosen to a seat in the parliament. When the old Diet adjourned in September 1906, its demise marked the beginning of the period when the vote of the people as a whole rather than that of a privileged class would determine the composition of the parliament and, consequently, the course of legislative effort. Universal suffrage had raised the number of voters from 126,000 (before the 1906 reform) to 1.27 million. When the new legislature was chosen, on the basis of the new law, eighty of its 200 members turned out to be Social Democrats, and twelve of the 200 were women.

The republican constitution of 1919 incorporated *in toto* the reforms of 1906. The single-chamber parliament and universal suffrage were carried over, without change, to the new fundamental law of independent Finland. An innovation was introduced in 1945, when the voting age was reduced from twenty-four to twenty-one years. Except for this change, these aspects of Finland's democratic institutions have withstood the test of time since well before World War I.

## Denmark

The history of representative self-government is briefer in Denmark than in Norway, Sweden, or Finland, and differs in many respects from that of her sister nations in the North. Although provincial and national assemblies had appeared in Denmark before 1600, they did not develop into representative bodies able to participate actively in legislation or in government and national affairs in general. Monarchy, unrestrained by constitutional limitations, had by 1660 become a royal absolutism destined to dominate the scene until well into the nineteenth century. The Danes were thus late in developing institutions and practices essential to democratic societies. The last century has more than sufficed to show, however, that Denmark's achievements in self-government have created a society no less free and progressive than that of the other Scandinavian democracies. It also demonstrated, interestingly enough, that nearly two centuries of royal absolutist tradition had not created insuperable obstacles to liberal change.

The introduction of royal absolutism in the seventeenth century is one of the most fascinating chapters in Danish annals. It was accomplished largely as the result of a disastrous war (1657-60) with

Sweden, which ended with substantial territorial cessions that gave Sweden her present southern boundaries and limited Denmark to Jutland and the islands that constitute Denmark today. The three years of war had an important effect upon the monarchy and upon the nobility, hitherto a powerful check upon the powers and pretensions of the Crown. King Frederick III emerged from the unsuccessful war a national hero while the nobility, which was blamed for Denmark's defeat, lost prestige and influence. In 1660, enjoying the support of the clergy and the burghers, the king succeeded in effecting a radical political change: the elective monarchy was made hereditary, the only condition being that the kingdom be kept indivisible and that the privileges of the various Estates be duly recognized.

The essential features of the new monarchy were defined by the so-called King's Law in 1665, which placed all powers in the hands of the king. The monarch, now above the law, was bound by only three limitations: he could not alter the King's Law, he could not decrease Denmark's area by cession of territory, and he had to abide faithfully by the Lutheran religion (the Augsburg Confession). Frederick III and his successors were thus endowed with powers greater than those enjoyed by any other ruler in Europe. The order introduced by the King's Law was not constitutionally changed until 1849. One of the reasons why the unlimited monarchy lasted as long as it did was that, after Frederick III died in 1670, the sovereigns of Denmark rarely abused their great powers. Nor did they prevent progressive measures, such as a significant agrarian reform in the 1780s, the introduction of provincial assemblies in the 1830s, and a reform of municipal governments in 1837. Although such improvements fell far short of satisfying the liberal elements, whose influence grew especially after 1840, they contributed to the gradual transformation of a society formerly markedly static.

By the opening of the 1840s, voices were increasingly raised in the press, in the provincial assemblies, and in the University demanding a constitution similar to the one drawn up at Eidsvoll for Norway. A particular goal of the liberals' program was a genuine national legislative assembly with the right to levy taxes and make changes in the electoral law. The Crown resisted these and other innovations, but several administrative reforms were carried through: a regular budget was introduced; parish and county councils were set up throughout the country; and Copenhagen, the capital, obtained a new municipal representative assembly—all measures that extended local self-government considerably beyond the limits set by the municipal law of 1837.

Slow though the progress was, the liberal elements were gaining ground. The king himself (Christian VIII, 1793-1848) had become constitutionally minded on the eve of the revolutionary year 1848; his successor, Frederick VII, announced a new constitution on January 28, 1848, ten days after his father's death. But the new constitution found no favor among the liberals and had not yet been accepted when the February revolution in France gave fresh hope to the liberal movement throughout Europe. During the next several months—a period punctuated by friction and war over the predominantly German-speaking duchies of Schleswig and Holstein—the problem of a constitution was shunted to the sidelines. It was not until June 5, 1849, that the "June Constitution" was adopted. It provided for a bicameral national legislature, the Rigsdag, which was to meet annually and to share with the king the right to enact laws, including measures relating to taxation and the allocation of funds. Although property and age qualifications for voting were defined in a manner that excluded the majority from the polls, freedom of assembly, press, association, and conscience was secured. The king was left with supreme authority in matters relating to national defense; he could also declare war, conclude peace, and make treaties. Thus the formal disappearance of an absolute monarchy dating from 1660 did not herald a sudden and complete introduction of modern democracy. In this regard, however, Denmark was no exception to the general rule at the time. Britain did not approach the one-man-one-vote stage until 1867 and 1884. France was the only European country to have manhood suffrage by 1849. The Danish "June Constitution" was a progressive—not to say radical—charter, and some of its consequences have invited the remark that it initiated a veritable though peaceful revolution.

The important gains recorded in 1849 nevertheless fell short of satisfying the spokesmen of the liberal movement. Further significant reforms did not come, however, until well after the turn of the century. Outstanding among them was that introduced in a proposal submitted to the legislature in 1912, which would have extended the right to vote to all men and women over twenty-five years of age, and also liberalized the upper house. The bill was defeated in the upper house by only two votes, but the effort was carried forward until a new Constitution Law was signed by the king on June 5, 1915. It provided that both houses of the legislature be elected by universal suffrage, women as well as men having the right to vote (the voting age for both was fixed at twenty-five years). The process of democratization was completed in 1953, when the upper house—long the object of attack by liberal and leftist groups—was abolished and Denmark accepted, as Norway and Finland had done earlier, a unicameral parliament. The voting age was reduced to twenty-one years in 1961.

## Sweden

The developments in Sweden differed in some respects from those in Denmark and Norway. The cession of Finland to Russia in 1809 brought about an internal political upheaval. In March of that year, in a coup d'état engineered by dissatisfied elements, King Gustavus IV was deposed. The provisional government that took charge summoned a meeting of the Riksdag and proceeded to draw up a new constitution to replace the autocratic fundamental law defined in 1772 and 1789. The new constitution, accepted on June 6, 1809, although frequently altered and elaborated since then, has remained the basis of Sweden's government for well over 150 years. It is the oldest written constitution in force in Europe, antedating Norway's by five years.

The new constitution vested executive power in the king ("The king shall alone rule the kingdom"). It provided that only the Riksdag and the king (jointly) could make or amend laws, and that the king's decisions required prior consultation with the Council of State (the members of which were appointed by the king). The members of the Council of State were answerable at law to the Riksdag for advice given; no cabinet or parliamentary responsibility, to be sure, was implied. The Riksdag had to be convened at least every fifth year, and among its powers was the right to control the administration of state finances. A special ordinance provided for the freedom of the press, and in the supreme court was vested the highest judicial authority in the land.

The constitution of 1809 did not change the composition and organization of the Riksdag: nobles, clergy, burghers, and peasants sat as separate chambers, as they had done since the seventeenth century. The Riksdag was strongly bureaucratic in character; except for the peasants, its members were for the most part civil or Crown servants. Also, neither the structure of the legislature nor the suffrage laws then in force made any allowance for the economic and social groups that had emerged since the Riksdag had been founded: important business groups, some categories of farmers, workers in towns, farm laborers, and the like were not represented. These and other shortcomings in the new constitutional order were eliminated only by later reforms.

Outstanding among these reforms was the reorganization of the Riksdag in 1865. Over forty proposals for changing the legislature had been presented during the two decades before the final solution of the question. The main supporters of the demand for change were the lower orders, the peasants and the burghers; during the 1859-60 session of the parliament, they petitioned that a new proposition for reform be presented. The nobles were resolutely opposed.

A new measure was prepared and introduced in the 1862-63 session of the Riksdag. A prolonged and heated discussion within and outside the legislature—numerous petitions and demonstrations testified to the interest of public opinion in the matter—preceded the final decision. On December 7, 1865, the House of Nobles accepted the measure by a vote of 361 to 294. The "unreformed" Riksdag had thus demonstrated the essence of orderly progress by voluntarily making room for a new and more liberally conceived national representation.

The parliament bill of 1865 provided for a Riksdag of two chambers, which was to meet annually. Members of the upper house were elected for a nine-year term by the provincial assemblies or the urban councils of the largest cities. Eligibility for seats in the upper chamber was restricted: members had to be thirty-five years of age or older and had to meet substantial property requirements. Members of the lower house were chosen directly by the voters for three-year terms. The new franchise provisions defined a property qualification for voting that severely restricted the size of the electorate. City workers and farm laborers were normally not entitled to vote; therefore large classes were still left without any representation. The main gainers by the new measures were the farmers, large numbers of whom henceforth qualified as voters. Not long after the 1865 reform, the Agrarian party emerged as the majority party in the second chamber.

The suffrage patterns defined in 1865 remained unchanged for many years. Although universal suffrage was demanded by the turn of the century by Social Democratic labor and the Liberal party, unrestricted male suffrage for elections to the lower house and the upper house did not become a fact until 1907 and 1918, respectively. In 1921, women got the right to vote and became eligible for seats in the Riksdag, on a footing of complete equality with men. The voting age was reduced from twenty-four to twenty-one years after World War II. The upper house is still elected by municipal and county electoral bodies (the members of which are elected by direct popular vote).

## The Rise of Parliamentary Government

The parliamentary system of government, with a cabinet—the real executive—formed of representatives of one or more parties holding a majority of the seats in the legislature, was much slower in coming in Scandinavia than the reform of the legislatures. Broadly speaking, the responsible, or cabinet, form of government emerged at about the time when the liberalization of the franchise established the one-man-one-vote rule. In Norway, Sweden, and Denmark, parliamentary government came only after prolonged and heated discussion and controversy; in Finland it was established, without extensive debate, by the fiat of the republican constitution of 1919. In the three monarchies, the position and prerogatives of the king complicated the problem and created marked differences of opinion regarding the powers of the citizenry and parliament on the one hand, and those of the monarch on the other. In pre-1917 Finland, the question was especially difficult because neither the legislature nor the government of the country could exert the kind of pressure or coercion on the Tsar-Grand Duke that the advocates of parliamentary government in the other Northern countries employed against their respective monarchs. The introduction of Finnish cabinets responsible to the legislature was therefore postponed until the nation had become independent.

The Norwegians were the first of the Scandinavians to free themselves from the preponderance of royal power implied by the king's right to appoint cabinet members, and by the fact that the ministers were responsible to the monarch and not to the parliament. The fact that the monarch was the king of Sweden (who was the king of Norway, in the view of most Norwegians, only in a secondary sense) gave the effort to reduce the power of the Crown and to center all real power in the Norwegian Storting an especially appealing nationalist coloration.

The idea that members of the Norwegian cabinet should sit in the legislature—without a vote, to be sure—had been put forth on numerous occasions since the early days of the union with Sweden. Nothing was accomplished, however, until the 1870s. Between 1878 and 1880, three successive Stortings passed an amendment to the Eidsvoll Constitution which provided for the seating of cabinet members in the parliament. The king vetoed the measure each time. The veto accompanying the last of the three attempts at amendment—the Storting had passed it on March 17, 1880—included the claim that, in matters relating to the constitution, the king had an absolute veto. The response of the Norwegian legislature was a resolution, accepted in June of the same year, stating that the amendment seating the ministers was a part of the fundamental law of the land and requesting that the cabinet promulgate it. A new premier was appointed by the king, and the Norwegian ministry—accepting the theory of royal veto power—ignored the June resolution of the Storting.

The legislature thereupon had recourse to impeachment as a means for enforcing its will. The premier and ten other members of the cabinet were impeached by the Odelsting and tried by a special high court composed of the supreme court and the members of Lagting. The defendants were found guilty: eight were condemned to loss of office and costs, three were only fined. The upshot of the conflict between king and parliament (the king was supported by a number of Norwegian conservatives) was the appointment, in July 1884, of a ministry headed by the majority leader in Norway's parliament, Johan Sverdrup. Parliamentary government had thus been carried through by a legislature stubbornly resolved to have its way. The Storting had become the main repository of governmental power, and a significant national victory had been recorded.

In Sweden the emergence and ultimate victory of parliamentary government spanned about a decade before 1917. It involved partly a gradual acceptance of English conceptions and practices regarding the dependence of cabinets upon parliamentary majority support, and partly a contest between the cabinet and the king that ended in a recognition of the principle that executive power reposes in the cabinet.

The Norwegian union crisis in 1905 led, among other things, to the convocation of an extraordinary Swedish Riksdag in June 1905, and the formation of a new national coalition government. The Riksdag proceeded at once to draft a program on the basis of which, it was hoped, the union problem could be satisfactorily solved. The program was entrusted to the new cabinet. The situation that had thus emerged meant that the cabinet was politically responsible, in the literal sense of the term, to the legislature. It was, therefore, the first instance in Sweden of a parliamentary government. Although the next several cabinets after 1905 neither were formed on nor functioned as the English model, the precedent set in 1905 contributed to the development that led, in 1917, to an open recognition that only cabinets responsible to the legislative branch would be accepted by the Riksdag and the nation.

The man largely responsible for this development was the leader of the Liberal coalition party, Karl Staaf. Staaf, a member of the 1905 emergency cabinet, became prime minister later in the year. The main problem that faced the Staaf ministry was Staaf's proposal to liberalize the franchise by introducing general manhood suffrage for elections to the lower house. Staaf was a firm believer in parliamentary government along English lines. He assumed that the proposed liberalization of the right to vote would place all real power of decision in the lower house and lead to the parliamentary system. The lower house accepted his program, but the upper house rejected it. True to his conception of the importance of parliamentary support for a functioning cabinet, Staaf resigned in 1906.

Staaf was called upon to head a second cabinet in 1911. His predecessor, whose party had suffered a substantial defeat in the 1911 election, had resigned, thus illustrating recognition of the principle Staaf had followed in 1906.

By 1914, Staaf found himself facing another test of the position and importance of the cabinet in Sweden's governmental scheme. The problem that posed the test was that of national defense. Defense expenditures and related matters had been hotly debated in and out of the Riksdag for some time before 1914. Social Democrat labor and liberal elements were opposed to what they considered to be excessive budget appropriations for the military establishment, while other groups—not all of which were conservative—agitated for armaments they considered essential for the nation's security. The Staaf cabinet failed to act in the matter speedily enough to satisfy those demanding "adequate" defense. They therefore arranged a massive demonstration to show that the people supported armaments expenditures and stood ready to shoulder the additional burdens involved. In February 1914, some 30,000 farmers marched to Stockholm to assure King Gustav of their readiness to support improved defenses. The king's speech, expressing his sympathy with the demands of the demonstrators, deviated sharply from the attitude of the Staaf cabinet and had been drafted without consultation with the cabinet. It was interpreted, especially by Liberals and Social Democrats, as an unwarranted intervention by the monarch (who was actually not attempting to assert any new powers but only expressing concern in a matter close to the hearts of many Swedes) and led to the resignation of the cabinet. The outbreak of World War I a few months later changed the situation overnight and led to a political truce that lasted until 1917. The truce enabled the Conservative ministry that had succeeded Staaf's to carry on for three full years.

The autumn elections in 1916 set the stage for the collapse of the political truce, giving the second chamber a considerable left-wing majority. Facing mounting attacks by the leftists, the Conservative cabinet resigned in March 1917. After a brief tenure in office by a moderate Conservative government, a new coalition government on a broad democratic basis was formed under the leadership of the Liberal, Nils Edén. His cabinet, composed of seven Liberals and four Social Democrats, is considered to mark the real beginning of parliamentary government in Sweden. Parliamentary government, however, frequently turned out to mean, especially before the mid-1930s, minority rather than majority governments: by 1928, no less than six ministries lacking majority support in the legislature had held office and led the nation during the crucial postwar decade.

The emergence of responsible government in Denmark was also marked by a prolonged contest between progressive and conservative elements. By 1872 the party of the farmer groups, the United Left, had won a majority of the seats in the lower house but could rely on only a few supporters in the upper chamber. The Crown-supported cabinet and public authority in general met evidences of radicalism and socialism (both appeared in the early 1870s) with stern measures but could not prevent the disaffected elements in the lower house from opposing the conservative government. The Liberals and related groups held a majority in that house continuously for twenty-nine years (1872-1901) before the first Liberal cabinet was formed in 1901. An indication of the lay of the land, and of the stubborn resistance of the upper house and the conservatives in general to political change, was the Estrup ministry. It held office for an exceptionally long time (1875-94) despite the fact that it was opposed by a solid majority in the lower chamber. The failure to heed the mandate delivered repeatedly in national elections by voters who were still relatively limited in numbers (universal suffrage was not introduced until 1915) continued for several years after the Estrup cabinet. It ended only in 1901, when the Liberal J. H. Deuntzer government took office.

The change in 1901 implied a repudiation of the right of the king, stated in the constitution and hitherto taken for granted, to select his ministers freely without heeding the preferences of the legislature in general or those of the lower house in particular. The Deuntzer ministry did not, however, mark a clear recognition of the superiority of the lower chamber over the upper house and therefore did not mean acceptance of the basic principle of parliamentary government. The new order of things was introduced by a constitutional amendment, carried through in 1915, which abolished the special electoral privileges of the upper house and transferred the balance of power to the lower chamber. The last stage in the development then recorded came in 1953, when all the political parties joined hands in enacting a constitutional change that abolished the upper house.

The process of democratization in Scandinavia during the past two generations or more has meant, among other things, that the personal political power of the monarch, including the right to appoint and dismiss members of the cabinet, has vanished. In this respect, Denmark, Norway, and Sweden—though monarchies—are equal to republican Finland, where the president is bound by the requirements of parliamentary government. The victory of democracy has also meant the elimination of property qualifications for voting. The extension of the rights to vote to women introduced an egalitarian aspect to political life that sets the past half-century sharply apart from earlier periods when privileges of classes or individuals were still dominant aspects of politics and government.

# FIVE

# POLITICAL PARTIES AND PROGRAMS

## Common Patterns and Developments

Political parties and party programs show a broad common pattern in the four Scandinavian countries. In each, five major parties dominate the scene: although they function under various party designations, they may be listed as Conservatives, Agrarians, Liberals, Social Democrats, and Communists. The minor parties are, for the most part, peripheral, although some of them are of greater importance than their numerical strength suggests. Because the membership of even the larger parties does not account for more than a fraction of the number of votes cast for them in national elections, electoral statistics give a partly misleading picture of party size. The discrepancy between votes obtained and party membership varies, but generally party members account for 10-40 per cent of the voters who go to the polls. Participation in elections is, by tradition, widespread. The number of voters normally includes 70-80 per cent of the qualified voters. (In the Swedish 1960 election the figure was 85.9 per cent; in the Finnish 1962 election, 85.1 per cent.)

The history of political parties and governments in Scandinavia underlines the marked stability and absence of crises characteristic of these countries. Political landslides are unknown. Although the unusual situation created by the war years 1939-45 gave the Communists, for example, an advantage denied them by normal circumstances, the electoral choices of the voters usually decree only minor changes in the distribution of seats in the legislature. The multiparty situation and the workings of the system of proportional representation prevent any sharp swings of the political pendulum. In recent years, the strength of Social Democrat labor—especially in Norway, Sweden, and Denmark—has acted as a stabilizing factor despite the fact that the Socialists have not yet captured a majority of the votes.

The 1930s witnessed certain deviations from normal political trends in the North. These were caused, to a considerable degree, by the economic difficulties that appeared after 1929, and they involved farmer groups more than industrial labor.

In the spring of 1931, in the midst of the depression, a rural people's movement emerged in southeastern Norway. Basically a distressed debtors' movement, its program demanded a moratorium on mortgage payments, a reduction of interest rates, and the prevention of mortgage-foreclosure sales of farms. The movement was relatively successful during 1932 and the early part of 1933; in some parts of the country forced sales were effectively boycotted. But it failed in its attempt to exert pressure on the political parties before the national elections in 1933, and to persuade the legislature in May to prohibit all forced sales and to declare a general moratorium on mortgage payments. The leaders of the movement thereupon turned for support to the Quisling-led Nasjonal Samling (National Union) the Norwegian Nazi organization, at the time hardly worthy of being called a party. In the 1933 elections the rural people's movement presented a joint ticket with Quisling's Nasjonal Samling in five districts. None of their candidates came near being elected. Quisling's party remained wholly unimportant through the 1930s and failed to receive more than insignificant support during the years of Nazi occupation (1940-45).

The record of Communism in Norway, although in all likelihood aided by the conditions created by the depression of the 1930s, is not impressive. In 1936, the Communists polled 4376 votes and failed, by a substantial margin, to capture a seat in the Storting. In the first postwar election in 1945, they received 176,500 votes and sent eleven representatives to the legislature. The modest Communist "tide" receded steadily thereafter. In 1953, only 90,400 voters out of a total of 1,779,800 preferred Communist candidates, three of whom gained seats in parliament. In 1957, only one Communist captured a seat; in 1961, the party failed to elect a single representative.

In Denmark, the depression produced a discontented farmers' organization the efforts and purposes of which corresponded, broadly speaking, to those of the rural people's movement in Norway. It failed, however, to persuade the voters that the goals it sought deserved national support. The discontented Danish farmers thereupon formed a working alliance in 1940 with Fritz Clausen and his unimportant Danish Nazi party. The results of the new affiliation were disappointing and convincingly demonstrated that Nazi political philosophy and goals were repulsive and foreign to the great majority of Danes. In the November 1932 election, the Nazis obtained 757 votes out of a total of 1,547,100 votes cast; in October 1935, they polled 16,250 votes out of a total of 1,646,500; in April 1939, they won 31,000 votes out of a total of 1,699,900 and seated their first representatives in the lower house (three seats out of a total of 148). The most conspicuous indication of the weakness of the Nazi cause came in the March 1943 election: although Denmark was under German military occupation at the time, the Nazi party obtained only 43,300 votes out of 2,010,800 cast and again captured only three seats in the lower house. Neither the discontented farmers before 1939 nor the German occupation after 1940 proved able to make the Nazi party more than a minor and transitory aspect of Danish political life.

The performance of the Communist party in Denmark has been basically the same as that elsewhere in the North. In no election between 1920 and 1932 did Communists receive more than a fraction of the votes cast in national elections. The largest number of votes —6219—were won in 1924, when 1,282,900 Danes went to the polls. Two Communists were elected to the lower house in 1932 and three in 1939, when some 41,000 Danes found the Communist creed and program congenial to their taste. In the first postwar election in 1945, 255,250 Communist votes were cast—enough to send eighteen representatives to the lower house. The party lost ground rapidly thereafter. In 1947, it captured nine seats; by 1957, the figure had dropped to six, and in the 1960 election, the Communists—with only 27,356 votes out of a total of 2,431,300 cast—failed to seat a single member in the legislature. The party held one seat in the upper house in 1947-51, but has had none since then.

In Finland, developments somewhat analogous to those in Norway and Denmark were recorded after 1930. In the early stages, they were connected with a widespread protest against the Communists. The Communist party had become the political home of many a Finnish radical who stood indicted before public opinion for participation in the Red Revolt in 1918. Several of them had escaped to Russia and continued to serve their cause from a foreign base. In the 1920s, the courts pronounced the Communist party a treasonous political organization in the service of a foreign power; nevertheless, the party had remained active, under various party labels, throughout the decade. In 1930, in response to pressure exerted especially but by no means exclusively by farmer groups, the legislature formally outlawed the party. The party thereupon went underground and was out of sight through the 1930s. One of the consequences of these developments was the appearance in 1933 of a new party, the Patriotic People's Movement. In many respects radically conservative, it included outright Fascist elements in its ranks. Its influence, however, remained limited: in the 1936 election, it captured fourteen of the 200 seats in the legislature; in 1939, only eight.

The political soil of Sweden offered only the most limited opportunities for political extremism. During the interwar years, Nazi or Fascist ideology failed to capture more than a handful of followers, and the national parliament was never called upon to accommodate devotees of either Mussolini or Hitler. Communism fared only little better. Throughout the 1930s, the 230-seat lower chamber had from eight to eleven Communist members, and although the years after 1945 gave Communism a temporary advantage, the highwater mark of the party's strength came after the 1948 election; a modest eight seats in the lower house and three seats in the 150-member upper house. By 1952, the lower chamber had only five Communists; the figure remained unchanged ten years later and rose only to eight in 1964. The Swedish electorate has thus demonstrated almost complete immunity to the totalitarian philosophies and practices sponsored by Moscow.

The decline of Communism in Scandinavia since the mid-1940s has no doubt been caused by many factors. Outstanding among them appear to be Soviet aggression in general, and especially the broad area of westward penetration represented by the satellite nations. The Communist coup in Czechoslovakia in 1948, the earlier Communist takeover in Poland, the fate of the three Baltic republics (Estonia, Latvia, and Lithuania), together with other evidences of the Kremlin's resolve to carry forward the revolutionary purposes defined by the Third International as early as 1919, suffice to account for much—if not all—of Scandinavia's postwar aversion to Communism. This feeling of aversion, and the more realistic understanding of the implications of Moscow's postwar policies, account for the failure of the Communists in Finland to gain ministerial seats since 1948. The exclusion of the Communists from cabinet posts is clear evidence of the change wrought by the developments of the past two decades. Although Communism in Finland has not been arrested at the same low level as in Denmark, Norway, and Sweden—the Communists have held 24-27 per cent of the seats in the 200-member legislature—its status and significance have shrunk to a degree that few could have predicted during the years immediately after the war.

One of the most striking features of Scandinavian politics and government over the past few decades is the prominence of the Social

Democratic party in the national legislatures and in the council chambers of state. Before 1914, the Socialists had become the largest single party only in Finland. By the early 1930s, however, the Social Democrats had become—in some respects—the leading party in all four countries; after the mid-1930s, socialism became a major factor on the Scandinavian political scene.

Scandinavian socialism originally developed according to the theories furnished by Marx, Engels, and the other German socialist luminaries. By the 1920s, however, something new had been added to the original exposition of the socialist program and purposes: revisionism or gradualism was accepted, on the whole, as a basic feature of socialism. The concept of class war and revolution as the only real midwife of "socialist" progress had been largely abandoned; reform and improvement had taken precedence over the concept of a cataclysmic revolution. A second conspicuous characteristic of Scandinavian socialism—especially in Finland, Norway, and Sweden—was its importance in nonindustrial, rural areas: Social Democracy has been markedly successful in obtaining the support of agricultural labor, and of small farmers and tradespeople as well. This is particularly true of the northern districts, where small land-holders frequently depend on nonagricultural part-time work and where, consequently, the line separating industrial workers from farmers is far from sharply drawn.

The role of post-1918 revisionist socialism in Scandinavia is revealed in election statistics. In Denmark, 389,650 Socialist votes were cast in 1920, giving the party forty-eight of the 148 seats of the lower house; in 1932, the corresponding figures were 660,800 and sixty-two; in 1935, they reached 759,100 and sixty-eight. The years between 1935 and 1952 witnessed some losses of Socialist strength, but elections after 1953 reversed the trend. In the September 1953 election, the Social Democrats received 836,500 votes out of a total of 2,166,400, and captured seventy-four seats in the legislature, which by then had become a 175-seat unicameral body. In November 1960, the Social Democrats received 1,024,000 votes (the total vote was 2,431,300) and sent seventy-six representatives to the parliament. Before the upper house was abolished in 1953, the Social Democrats had held between thirty-eight and forty-two out of the seventy-six seats of the chamber for nearly two decades.

Norway illustrated the same general trend. In 1936, Socialist labor registered 618,600 votes of the 1,455,200 cast, and captured seventy of the 150 seats. In 1945, when the Communists were challenging

the Social Democrats in the attempt to garner leftist votes, the Socialists succeeded in getting seventy-six seats in the parliament. In
the 1953 election, by which time the postwar backlash against Communism was already in evidence, the Socialists were supported by
830,450 votes out of 1,779,800 cast, giving the party seventy-seven
seats. This narrow majority was maintained in 1957, when the party
obtained seventy-eight seats. Some ground was lost, however, in September 1961, when the party polled 855,500 votes out of a total of
1,791,100 and had to be satisfied with only seventy-four representatives.

The result of the 1961 election posed an interesting question: Inas-
much as Socialist labor had failed to receive a majority, should the
Socialist-led Einar Gerhardsen cabinet continue in office? It was
answered in an interesting way. In October, after it had assessed the
political situation, the Socialist party's national committee decided
that a coalition with the non-Socialist parties was not in order; that
the non-Socialist parties were "in the minority" in the parliament
(not counting two dissidents, they held seventy-four seats, the same
number captured by the Socialists); that a non-Socialist Cabinet was
not "a natural solution in the present situation"; and that therefore
the Socialist ministry must be ready and willing to continue in office.
Thus the Gerhardsen cabinet continued to govern the country, and
national domestic and foreign policies—clearly defined for several
years—were carried forward without interruption.

In Sweden, where the main political arena is the lower house, Social
Democracy has also been a leading force for many years and a nearly
dominant factor since the mid-1940s. In the first postwar election in
1948, the Social Democrats received 1,789,500 votes out of a total of
3,875,600 cast, and captured 112 of the 230 seats of the lower chamber. In the upper house they held, in the same year, eighty-five out of
150 seats. The 1952 election reduced their representation to 110 seats
in the lower house. In 1956 they polled 46.2 per cent of the votes and
again seated 112 representatives in the lower house. The 1960 election raised their figure to 116. The Socialists' actual voting strength,
however, was only 115 or exactly one half of the lower-house membership (the Speaker has no vote). The failure to obtain a clear majority in the house, however, has not prevented the party from controlling the legislative branch and providing the country with a Socialist cabinet as well.

The Finnish Socialist party began with conspicuous electoral successes immediately after the parliamentary and suffrage reform of

1906. The first election after universal suffrage had been introduced (1907) gave the Socialists eighty of the 200 seats in the parliament, and by 1913, the figure had been raised to ninety. In 1916, under exceptional wartime conditions, the Socialists captured 103 seats and thereby obtained majority control of the legislature. They lost this temporary advantage in 1917, but remained the leading party through the 1920s and the 1930s. The Communist party robbed the Socialists of some of their strength in 1922-29, but after the elections of 1933, 1936, and 1939, Social Democracy held from seventy-eight to eighty-five seats and again stood forth, by a substantial margin, as the largest party in the country.

The years since the end of World War II have witnessed a marked decline of Socialist strength in Finland. Two main reasons account for the changed status of the party. The first is the Communist party—or, rather, The Democratic Peoples' League (the SKDL), composed of Communists and fellow travelers, through which the Communists have operated since 1945. The SKDL has drawn considerable support from the groups that previously voted the Social Democratic ticket. In the 1945 election, the Socialists were reduced to fifty seats while the SKDL obtained forty-nine; in the 1948 election, the figures were fifty-four and thirty-eight; and in 1958, forty-eight and fifty. Since 1958, the party has suffered from internal dissension and divisions that have further weakened it. After the 1962 election, its representatives in the legislature were reduced to thirty-eight; the SKDL captured forty-seven seats. Although the 1963-64 developments indicated that Social Democratic party unity would be re-established in the near future, the party will probably not recover all the ground lost during the past two decades. It remains, however, the only gradualist workers' party in Finland and, as such, it is an object of particular Communist hatred and opposition.

## Social Democracy and Government

The real test of the importance of the Social Democratic party is its capacity to offer the nation labor-led cabinets. In recent decades Socialist cabinets have been the rule, rather than the exception, in Scandinavia. Sweden's first Social Democratic government took office in 1920; Denmark's, in 1924; Finland's, in 1926; and Norway's, in 1928. None of the Socialist-led Cabinets before the mid-1930s commanded majority support in their respective legislatures. They existed on the sufferance of non-Socialist parliamentary majorities that chose temporarily to give their support to Socialist-led governments for reasons that seemed satisfactory, for the time being, to the majority groups. After 1935, however, the situation changed. Socialists were increasingly called upon to assume responsibility—alone or in cooperation with agrarian and other groups—for the formulation of national policy. In none of the Scandinavian countries had the Social Democrats carried over 50 per cent of the popular vote when their new prominence was thrust upon them. Their success in assuming national leadership before World War II therefore depended on the fact that the citizenries of these democracies stood ready to accept a sensible interpretation of the outcome of electoral contests: despite the Socialists' failure to obtain clear majority support, the verdict of the national elections was not challenged by the groups or parties that had failed to persuade the voters.

In Sweden, the Social Democrats formed their first—minority—cabinet in 1920 and remained in office until 1923, when a Conservative ministry took over. The Socialists held office for a second time in 1924-26, again as a minority cabinet. Liberal and Conservative cabinets alternated during the next half-dozen years. In 1932 the Social Democrats formed a government and remained in office until 1936, when they formed a coalition government with the Farmers' Union. In 1939, with the outbreak of the war, the coalition, headed by Social Democrat Per Albin Hansson, was expanded to include all parties except the Communist. Since 1945 (except for a brief interlude in 1951), the Socialists have headed and manned the cabinet. Perhaps the best way of indicating the extent of Social Democratic leadership in Sweden is to note that Premier Hansson guided his country's destinies for fourteen years before he died in 1946, and that his successor, Tage Erlander, has served as prime minister since then. The two Socialist premiers thus represent over three decades of Social Democracy in the seat of power.

The multiparty system is more sharply etched in Finland than in Sweden. This circumstance, the fact that the Social Democratic party suffered for many years from its association with the Red Revolt in 1918, and the failure of the Socialists to obtain a majority in the legislature, account for the absence of prominent Socialist leadership in the cabinets of 1919-39. During the two decades, only one Socialist ministry held office, in 1926-27. It was a minority cabinet, for the Socialists held only sixty seats in the parliament. During the late 1930s, the Socialists held portfolios in three cabinets: one was headed by a member of the Agrarian party; two, by members of the Progressive party.

The multiparty aspect of Finnish politics since 1945 has perpetuated the rule of coalition cabinets. Nineteen governments held office between November 1944 and the spring of 1962. Of the nineteen, one was a Social Democrat (minority) cabinet, two were coalition ministries headed by a Social Democrat prime minister, and seven others had Social Democrat ministers. The most recent Socialist-led government held office in August-December 1958. The cabinets since 1958 have included no Social Democrats; instead they have been dominated by the Agrarian party, which, over the past several years, has contended that Socialists in the ministry would mean difficulties with the Soviet Union (long inclined to view Finnish Socialists with particular suspicion, not to say enmity).

Laborite cabinets and ministers have been commonplace in Danish political life for some four decades. The first Social Democrat ministry, headed by Premier Thorvald Stauning, was appointed in 1924. Because it included several non-Socialists, it was not a genuine Socialist government, and the Socialists—not having a majority in the legislature—were dependent upon support from other groups. Economic difficulties, particularly a crisis in agriculture in 1926, caused an election in 1926 and the resignation of the Stauning government. The 1929 election gave the laborites a majority in the lower house and led to another Stauning-led cabinet. Social Democrats, under Stauning's leadership, retained control of the lower chamber for the next decade. The normal political and party situation was changed overnight by the German occupation of Denmark in April 1940. Immediately after the country's liberation in May 1945, the nation went to the polls to elect a new parliament.

The 1945 election gave the Social Democrats 32.8 per cent of the vote: forty-eight out of the 148 seats in the lower house and thirty-four of the seventy-eight seats in the upper chamber. This was a serious setback for the Socialists because the Communists, who received 12.5 per cent of the votes and eighteen seats in the legislature, drew practically all their strength from normally Social Democratic voters. The Socialists recouped part of their losses in the 1947 election: they got 40 per cent of the votes and fifty-seven seats in the lower house; the Communists received only nine seats. In 1953, the Socialists captured sixty-one seats; the Communists, seven. In a second election in September of the same year, the Social Democrats received seventy-four out of the 179 seats in the enlarged single-chamber legislature (introduced by means of a constitutional amendment in 1953); and the Communists, eight. (Two of the 179 seats are assigned to Greenland and two to the Faroe islands.)

The general election in May 1957 reduced Socialist representation from seventy-four to seventy (and Communist seats from eight to six). The Socialist setback sufficed to bring about the resignation of Premier H. C. Hansen. The result was a coalition cabinet, again headed by Premier Hansen, composed of nine Socialists, four Social Liberals and three Single-Taxers; the coalition held ninety-three seats in the parliament and thus gave the new government assurances of comfortable parliamentary support. The 1960 election resulted in the elimination of the Single-Taxers from the legislature and in a new coalition government led by Social Democrat V. Kampmann, whose party colleagues held all but three of the eleven ministerial portfolios.

In Norway also laborite ministers and cabinets have been the rule, not the exception. The Social Democrats slowly gained in influence after 1903, when they first obtained representation in the Storting. Severely mauled by the emergence of extreme radicalism that spawned the Norwegian Communist party in 1923, the Socialists did not begin to close ranks until 1927. The first labor government was formed in 1935. The date marks the beginning of a laborite rule that has continued, with but a minor interruption during the last war and another in 1963, down to the present. The verdict of the electorate during the past decade has perpetuated the choice of the years before 1940-45 and after: labor has been repeatedly returned to power. In 1953, the party received somewhat less than 50 per cent of the votes but captured seventy-seven of the 150 seats in the legislature. The election of 1957 delivered seventy-eight seats to the party and kept Prime Minister Einar Gerhardsen and his colleagues in office. The next election year, 1961, marked the twenty-sixth year of Social Democratic government in the country. It witnessed a small decline in laborite strength, but no general repudiation of Social Democracy: Premier Gerhardsen's party received seventy-four seats—two less than a majority. The Gerhardsen cabinet remained in office, however, on the grounds that the opposition was in no position to obtain a majority. Labor has carried on since 1961, despite some minor difficulties, under the able leadership of Premier Gerhardsen (whose cabinet experience goes back to 1945).[1]

---

[1] The Gerhardsen cabinet suffered its first defeat in twenty-eight years when the Storting voted, on August 23, 1963, to adopt a motion of no confidence.

Scandinavian Social Democratic parties and programs have long since openly repudiated or silently abandoned some of their earlier goals and purposes. Swedish Socialists no longer contend that the monarchy should be abolished; they accept the monarchy as a natural and congenial part of the existing order and concern themselves with matters that are of real substance and meaning in a modern democracy. The Danish Social Democratic party convention in Copenhagen, meeting in June 1961, rejected (with but one dissenting vote) the idea of a republican constitution and a proposal for the separation of church and state. Similar changes in party attitude have emerged in Norway. In republican Finland, other indications of the rejection of the militant attitudes of yesteryear have been recorded for decades.

Another indication of the new moderation of the Socialists is their attitude toward the socialization of national resources and means of production in general. Doctrinaire considerations no longer dictate the Socialists' verdict on questions of state control or ownership of important resources of industrial enterprises; practical matters—such as the needs of national defense, the conservation of natural resources, and the availability or lack of capital—are the deciding factors. Questions in this field are decided ad hoc on their merits and not on the basis of rules drawn from a handbook of Marxist theory.

Still another characteristic of Scandinavian Social Democracy is the surprising fact that it is not a genuine majority party. Broadly speaking, the Social Democrats have been at the helm for over a generation, yet they have not succeeded in persuading the voters to deliver a clear majority vote in their favor. To date, the maximum electoral support given the Social Democrats has not exceeded 50 per cent, although they have on several occasions captured (primarily because of the operation of proportional representation) more than half of the seats in the legislature. In late years Socialist strength has seemingly leveled off close to the 50 per cent mark, and the voters appear to resist all efforts to increase the figure by a margin large enough to give the party real majority support.

Readiness to cooperate with "bourgeois" parties has likewise become a part of the Socialist record in Scandinavia, especially since the 1930s. The principle of "no traffic with the capitalist enemy," embraced in the early years of Scandinavian socialism, has gone the way of all earthly things. Cooperation with the Agrarian parties has

The non-Socialist coalition government, headed by the leader of the Conservative party, John Lyng, that succeeded the laborite cabinet remained in office for less than a month and was followed by another labor cabinet.

been particularly common. In all four countries, the years since the 1930s have offered telling illustrations of cooperation between the two parties, although other party coalitions have also functioned. In Denmark, Social Democratic governments held office in 1947-50 and in 1953-57 with the support of the small land-holder Social Liberals (who did not, incidentally, hold any ministerial portfolios). In 1957, the Socialists, the Social Liberals, and the Single-Taxers joined hands in forming a coalition cabinet under a Social Democratic prime minister. The cabinet was the first since 1945 to enjoy the support of a genuine majority in the legislature. In Finland, two of the post-1948 Socialist-led coalition cabinets were composed of three non-Social Democrats. The cabinet headed by Socialist Premier K. A. Fagerholm in 1958 included a representative of the conservative National Coalition party. Sweden and Norway have illustrated the same capacity for political accommodation, although labor has been able to rely, in both countries, upon near-majority strength.

This strength has led some Swedish non-Socialist party leaders, in recent years, to propose the formation of a common party or coalition that could be counted upon to obtain enough support in national elections to dislodge the Socialists from the seats of power. The proposals have produced no concrete results as yet, and the indications are that Social Democracy will not be called upon to contend against a united "bourgeois" party front. Meantime, the general political situation in Sweden and the other nations of the North continues to rest upon and to demand readiness and capacity for compromise and accommodation. The capacity for compromise, dictated by circumstances seemingly beyond the control of any single party, is the best and probably the only guarantee that workable solutions for national problems will be fashioned in a manner that not only satisfies the party or parties in power but is also congenial to the large minorities that constitute a continuing "loyal opposition." [2]

[2] The readiness to compromise has not, however, been developed to the point where political generosities hold full sway. Prideful claims to party virtues presumably denied by a discriminating Providence to other parties are by no means uncommon. For example, during the Swedish September 1964 election the Social Democrats tried to persuade the electorate that the Social Democratic party was responsible for the success in fighting poverty, eliminating slums, reducing unemployment, providing broadly defined social services and security, and other benefits. The Socialists ignored the fact that Liberals and other supporters of ameliorative policies labored on behalf of enlightened social legislation long before the Socialists reached their present prominence, and that impressive political, economic, and social emancipation of the common man has been recorded

Scandinavian political developments during the past few decades have been marked by the steady decline of the liberal parties that dominated the political arena before and shortly after World War I. One reason for their decline has unquestionably been the rise of the labor parties. Another reason, by no means unrelated to the first, is the gradual achievement of most—if not all—of the liberal program of a generation or two ago, and the acceptance of liberal purposes—implied by the victory of the program—by large groups of the citizenry that never enlisted under the liberal banner. Finally, the liberal cause has continued to be represented, even during the years of the liberal parties' decline, by individual liberal leaders of outstanding capacity and talent. For instance, in Finland, eight of the twenty cabinets between 1919 and 1939 were headed by members of the Progressive party. During these years the Progressives normally held only about ten to seventeen of the 200 seats in the legislature. This discrepancy between legislative strength and cabinet leadership reflected an aspect of pre-1939 Scandinavian politics that the realities of the years after 1945 have largely eliminated.

---

in other countries where socialism has played only a minor role, if any. The Scandinavian press yields abundant proof of the Socialists' inclination to claim much and to concede little.

# SIX

# SCANDINAVIA AND WORLD WAR II

Only one of the four Scandinavian countries—Sweden—escaped the scourge of World War II. Finland fell victim to unprovoked Soviet aggression; Denmark and Norway were forced to submit to the ruthless designs of Hitler and suffered five long years of German occupation. Even Iceland far out in the Atlantic became involved. Placed under British "protection" in 1940 and American control in 1941, the small nation escaped enemy occupation but nevertheless felt the effects of the war in ways destined to leave a deep impression upon the Icelanders for years to come.

World War II was launched when Hitler invaded Poland on September 1, 1939. The stage for the invasion had been set by a secret protocol attached to the Nazi-Soviet nonaggression pact of August 23, 1939. Germany and the Soviet Union had agreed that "in the event of a territorial and political rearrangement" in the areas belonging to Finland, Estonia, Latvia, and Lithuania, the northern boundary of Lithuania would divide the spheres of influence of the two signatories, and that "in the event of a territorial and political rearrangement" of the areas belonging to Poland, their spheres of influence were to be "bounded approximately by the line of the rivers Narev, Vistula, and San." Poland's future existence would be decided later "by means of a friendly agreement" between Germany and the Soviet Union. The events of September showed that the "territorial and political rearrangement" contemplated by the protocol was in fact carried through by the two signatories themselves.

Although the nonaggression pact caused a sensation and considerable unease, especially in the West—Britain and France were attempting at the time to enlist the Soviet Union in a common front against Hitler—it was seen by many Scandinavians in a more optimistic light. It was felt, particularly in Finland, that the treaty had assured the peace of the Baltic and Scandinavian area. Denmark had signed a nonaggression treaty with Germany in May 1939. Finland had a nonaggression treaty, in force until 1945, with the Soviet Union. These treaties, and the well-known neutrality policy of the Scandinavian states, appeared to justify the hope and conclusion that the threat to Scandinavia's peace had been reduced by the Hitler-Stalin pact. Their confident expectation was that their own good intentions would suffice to keep them out of war.

## Finland

Immediately after Poland was attacked, the Northern democracies proclaimed a common and unqualified neutrality policy. To lend dramatic emphasis to the occasion, the heads of state of the four nations met in a much-publicized conference that began in Stockholm on October 18th. Finland had already been exposed for two weeks to Soviet territorial demands and pressures. King Christian X of Denmark, King Haakon VII of Norway, King Gustav V of Sweden, and President K. Kallio of Finland met to demonstrate in an unmistakable manner their unqualified resolve to safeguard vital national interests by adhering to a policy of neutrality and their support of Finland's effort to meet recent Soviet demands on her territory. On the closing day of the Stockholm conference, King Gustav V of Sweden emphasized the determination of the four nations to avoid all involvement in the quarrels of the powers at war: each of the four countries, in full agreement with the others, would follow the tested and tried policy of "impartial neutrality to which all the states of the North have declared their allegiance." The peoples of the North, he declared, "are imbued with a desire, shared by all of them, to live in peace with all others. They are also inspired by a common determination to live as free nations."

Even before Hitler and Stalin had erased independent Poland from the political map of Europe, the Soviet Union undertook moves in Estonia, Latvia, and Lithuania that seemed ominous to the Scandinavians. From September 25th to October 5th the government representatives of the three republics were summoned to Moscow, one by one, and "persuaded" to accept arrangements that placed them, for all practical purposes, under Soviet control. Each "gave" the Soviet Union the right to occupy certain ports, air fields, and military installations, and to man them with Soviet forces. The occupation was to last for the duration of the war, allegedly for the purpose of aiding Soviet defenses. The three republics found but meager comfort in the provision, inserted into each of the treaties, that the agreements would "in no way" limit their sovereignty or their economic and political systems. The real meaning of these provisions was revealed in the summer of 1940, when the three nations were incorporated in the Soviet Union.

The Baltic agreements had barely been completed when it became clear that Scandinavia would not escape the attention of the Soviet Union. Finland received an invitation to send representatives to Moscow, and the recent developments in Estonia, Latvia, and Lithuania had given an indication of what the Kremlin had in mind when it suggested that certain "concrete political questions" would be discussed.

The discussions in Moscow began on October 7th. The Finns were asked to agree to substantial changes in Finland's southeastern boundary, involving the cession to the Soviet Union of certain territories and several islands in the Gulf of Finland, and the provision of a naval base in order "to strengthen the defenses of Leningrad." The Finns refused, insisting that Finland was unqualifiedly neutral, would under no circumstances violate Soviet territory, and could in no way be considered a threat to the security of its eastern neighbor. They also pointed out that the Soviet demands amounted to a threat to Finland's independence. After about a month of inconclusive exchanges, during which Moscow refused to abandon its demands but neither presented an ultimatum nor threatened war, the discussions ended—temporarily, the Finns assumed—on November 13th. The Soviet Union adopted a new tactic: in retaliation for a trumped-up border incident, the Soviet army invaded Finland on November 30th, apparently confident of a quick and complete victory.

The Finns, however, decided to resist. Still determined to do whatever could be done under the circumstances to re-establish peace, they immediately reorganized their government, hoping that a new cabinet would serve notice on the Soviet Union of their resolve to do everything possible short of abject surrender to end the war in its early stages. When it became clear that the purpose of the Soviet Union was to destroy the republic—as indicated by the setting up of a Soviet-sponsored "Finnish" government behind the Russian lines— the Finnish government attempted to enlist the aid of the League of Nations. The Soviet Union refused to appear before the League on the specious grounds that "the Soviet Union is not at war with Finland" and does not "threaten Finland with war" because it had "concluded on December 2nd a treaty of friendship and mutual assistance" with the "Finnish Democratic Republic" (the puppet government set up by the Soviet Union itself). The ruse deceived nobody. The Assembly of the League condemned the Soviet action and appealed to League members to extend "material and humanitarian aid" to Finland. On December 14th, the Council of the League stated that the actions of the Soviet Union had placed it outside the League—an indirect way of saying that the Soviet Union had ceased to be a member of the League of Nations.

The Russo-Finnish war lasted for over three months. By the time the peace treaty was signed (March 12, 1940), the Finns had astonished the world by their resolute and skillful defense against the invader. Convinced that the nation's independence was at stake, the Finns fought fiercely, although attempting all the while to obtain tolerable peace terms from the enemy. The behind-the-scenes negotiations, in which Sweden's good offices played an important part, ultimately led to a treaty which left intact the nation's independence and the people's freedom. Yet the price of freedom was high: southeastern Finland and other areas along the Soviet border, amounting to some 12 per cent of the nation's territory, were ceded to the Soviet Union; the Cape of Hanko, in the southwest, was "leased" to the Soviets for thirty years. These and other concessions meant the loss of about 12 per cent of Finland's economic resources. The casualties were high, too: 23,150 soldiers were killed in action; 43,550, wounded. The population of the ceded areas, about 420,000, chose to leave their homes and property and to move within the new borders of Finland. There they were provided, during the next few years, with new lands, homes, and jobs as quickly as the enactment of necessary new tax laws—including a steep capital levy ranging from 2.5 to 20 per cent—and other measures permitted.

Hitler's invasion of the Soviet Union in June 1941 led to the second phase of the Finnish-Soviet war. Immediately after the German attack began, Finland declared herself neutral and was recognized as neutral, for some days, by Britain and other nations. Soviet military operations against Finland, begun within hours of Hitler's attack, changed the situation and led to a Finnish declaration, on June 25th, that the country was once again at war. By December, the areas lost to the Soviet Union under the 1940 treaty had been recovered and Finnish forces had established favorable positions in Soviet Karelia. The front remained unchanged thereafter until the summer of 1944.

The Finns insisted that their war was not connected with the conflict between the Western Powers and Hitler. They were co-belligerents of Germany but not allies, and were bound by no treaty or agreement with Hitler. But the distinction Finland underscored became meaningless with the deterioration of the military situation: by the autumn of 1944, Finland had once again to accept Soviet terms. The terms were defined in an armistice agreement (signed on September 19, 1944) and ultimately embodied in the Peace Treaty of Paris (signed on February 10, 1947). They re-established the frontiers defined in the 1940 peace treaty and provided for the cession of Petsamo in the northeast (on the coast of the Arctic Ocean). The Hanko enclave was abandoned and another area, within a dozen miles of Helsinki, was substituted as a Soviet base. Among the other exactions imposed by the Soviet Union was a war indemnity of $300 million, to be paid in goods over a period of six years (the goods were to be valued in American gold dollar prices as of 1938, plus an increase of 10-15 per cent).

The enormous reparation payments—which continued until September 1952, the actual amount varyingly estimated at $600 million to $900 million—were only part of the cost paid by Finland for independence. The 1941-44 phase of the war cost the lives of 53,750 soldiers; the wounded numbered 59,500. Finland's withdrawal from the war in September 1944, because it involved acceptance of the obligation to oust the Germans, led to a war against the Germans stationed in northern Finland. This struggle lasted until April 1945. Finland thus was, for about half a year, a co-belligerent of the Western Powers and the Soviet Union. The Finnish campaign against the Germans, a minor aspect of the larger war and largely obscured by other developments in the vast conflict, meant additional huge losses for the Finns. Because of the scorched-earth policy systematically applied by the retreating Germans, roads, bridges, railroads, houses, and other kinds of property (later valued at about $120 million) were destroyed, adding to the costs of the war imposed on Finland by the aggression of the Soviet Union.

## Denmark

The German attack on Poland; the Soviet participation in the dismemberment of Poland; the Soviet moves shortly thereafter in Estonia, Latvia, and Lithuania; and the invasion of Finland more than sufficed to destroy the Scandinavians' hope that neutrality was an adequate shield against disaster.

The war was only a few weeks old when it became clear to Norway and Sweden that neutrality declared did not necessarily mean se-

curity achieved. During the Soviet-Finnish war in 1939-40, the Western Allies contemplated sending an expeditionary force, through
Norway and Sweden, to the beleaguered Finns. The main but hidden
purpose was to create a new front against Germany and to prevent
the shipment of Swedish iron ore to Germany. When approached
for rights of free transit of Allied troops and equipment to Finland,
both Norway and Sweden refused. The Allies, instead of proceeding
from persuasion to coercion, accepted the verdict—partly, it would
seem, because the Finns decided to accept Soviet terms rather than
face the risks involved in requesting and accepting Allied aid, thereby
becoming participants in the wider conflict. Whatever dangers in-
hered in the Allied intervention plans appeared to have been dis-
pelled by the conclusion of the Soviet-Finnish treaty on March 12,
1940. A few weeks later, however, Hitler's armies invaded Denmark
and Norway.

April 9, 1940, stands out as the day of infamy in the history of
Denmark and Norway. Both countries had been as prompt as Finland
and Sweden in declaring their neutrality immediately after the war
began. Their commitment to pacific policies and purposes had been
as unqualified as that of their Scandinavian sister nations. In Denmark, the dominant Social Democratic party had for the past decade
advocated complete Danish disarmament; in Norway, the Socialists
had given convincing evidence of their acceptance of pacifism and
their repudiation of war as an instrument of national policy. Both
countries looked forward to neutrality as an anchorage no less safe
during World War II than it had been in World War I.

Late in May 1939, when Hitler had already embarked on the
course that led to the invasion of Poland, he offered each of the
Scandinavian countries a nonaggression pact. Norway, Sweden, and
Finland politely refused. Denmark, more exposed to potential German moves, understandably decided to accept the offer. The pact
signed on May 31st stated, in part, that neither country would "under
any circumstances go to war and neither will they in any way resort
to force against each other." Ten months and nine days later (April 9,
1940), Hitler's armies launched an invasion of Denmark. The invasion was carried to a successful conclusion within a few hours. A
German ultimatum claiming that Germany had acted to protect
Denmark from a British invasion fooled nobody, and German assurances that Denmark's integrity and independence would be respected
and guaranteed appeared incongruous to most Danes in view of the
fact that both had already been violated by the invasion itself.

The events of the months after the invasion suggested that Hitler's plans called, not for a full military occupation and a puppet government, but for the setting up of a "model protectorate." Although questions and problems relating to military matters were placed at once under the supervision and control of a German general, the king and government were otherwise to function as usual. Before long, however, the relatively liberal treatment of the Danes changed. The country was increasingly turned into a base for operations against Britain, Danish military and naval equipment was taken over, extensive fortifications were built, and the small Danish army was disarmed in 1943. Meantime it was also becoming evident that the German promise not to interfere in the nation's internal affairs was worthless.

At the time of the invasion, the Danish government was headed by Thorvald Stauning, a veteran socialist who had served as premier in several cabinets since the spring of 1929. An old-line pacifist and Social Democrat, he had been a staunch advocate of Danish disarmament; now he had to witness a national humiliation that could be ended only by the use of military force superior to that of the Germans. Stauning believed that Germany would win the war, and that therefore everything possible must be done to secure Denmark's position in the new order. This could best be done by preventing Denmark from becoming a theater of war, by keeping intact the Danish legal system—the laws, the courts, and the administration of justice in general, and by preventing permanent damage to the nation's productive potential. These purposes could best be served by going as far as possible in trying to meet the German demands. Realistic adaptation to existing circumstances called for collaboration.

The five years of the occupation offered repeated tests of the Danes' adaptability and capacity for defining the limits of their accommodation of the Germans. Much had to be yielded between 1940 and 1945, but a great deal was saved. Despite German recommendations and pressures, and such coercive measures as the martial law introduced for over a month in August 1943, Danish conscription for German service was avoided; anti-Jewish legislation on the German model was courageously refused; the introduction of the German naval code and procedures was rejected; a customs and monetary union with Germany, involving a definition of citizenship giving Danes and Germans equal rights in both countries, was prevented; and, despite mounting difficulties and the Germans' increased use of force, the spirit of protest and opposition grew rather than diminished. Sabotage, strikes, and an efficient underground resistance movement (sustaining, among other things, an illegal press of astonishing vitality) testified to the strength and resourcefulness of the hard-pressed Danes. Arrests and executions merely steeled the national will to fight for the day of liberation.

At the center of the resistance movement stood the Danish Free-dom Council. Established in 1943 on Constitution Day (June 5th), it proceeded to coordinate "representatives of all Danish movements that desire, in agreement with the will of the people, actively to fight" the German occupation "until Denmark is again a free and inde-pendent country." Its membership was drawn from a broad segment of the Danish citizenry: at its last meeting, after the liberation of Denmark, the Council's leadership included two professors, one for-eign service officer, two newspaper editors, and one farmer ("land-owner"). It rendered invaluable service in preparing the nation for D-Day and in planning for the tasks that awaited the country after liberation. When British troops entered Denmark after the German capitulation on May 5, 1945, the transition to peaceful conditions began at once. By that time, the Freedom Council had some 43,000 fighters ready to do their part in carrying Denmark back to the con-stitutional and democratic order.

*Norway*

Norway, under Nazi occupation in 1940-45, fared worse than Den-mark. The main reason was Norway's establishment of a lawful, con-stitutional government-in-exile in Britain, and the stubborn refusal of the overwhelming majority of Norwegians to ignore or repudiate that government.

The German invasion of Norway was slower and costlier than the simultaneous invasion of Denmark. Norwegian resistance to the enemy continued for two months; fighting did not end until June 10th. During the two-month war, the Allies made an unsuccessful attempt to aid the Norwegians, but were forced to withdraw their fighting units, including planes and ships, late in May. Although the resolute and skillful struggle of the Norwegians failed to repel the Germans, it prevented them from capturing the king and the govern-ment. On June 7th, King Haakon V boarded a British warship and sailed for London, accompanied by the cabinet, which was headed by Laborite Johan Nygaardsvold (it had been hastily enlarged by the ap-pointment to portfolios of three representatives of other parties, in order to make it a truly national government) and other leading personages, including members of the military staff. The gold reserves of the Bank of Norway were also saved and sent to Britain. Because of the size of the Norwegian merchant marine (4.8 million tons), some 80 per cent of which served the Allied cause, its earnings were large enough to enable the Norwegian government-in-exile to support the resistance to the enemy at home and to build up and maintain a considerable fighting force that became part of the Allied war machine.

Having failed to capture the legal government, the Germans attempted to set up a pliant puppet government—but the effort was unsuccessful. The Germans thereupon established, in September 1940, an undisguised Nazi rule. They made use of Nazi turncoats such as Vidkun Quisling (his name was destined to become a synonym for *traitor*), who was later executed for treason. The number of Norwegians ready to follow Quisling or the Germans remained small throughout the five years of galling and costly occupation. Meanwhile, the resistance movement and the cause of freedom enlisted the sympathies and support of the nation. Despite extensive material spoliation (the staggering costs of the occupation are suggested by the fact that the national debt was increased ninefold by 1945), systematic efforts to Nazify the people, and the use of imprisonment, torture, execution, concentration camps, and a general policy of terror, the home front held fast. When the day of liberation came (May 8, 1945), the people of Norway were ready to proceed to the task of setting their own house in order.

The king and the government-in-exile returned to Norway on June 7, 1945, and temporary arrangements were made at once for the governance of the country at the national and local levels. The Nygaardsvold cabinet resigned on June 12th, according to the premier's earlier promise that his government would leave office as soon as Norway had been freed. It was succeeded by a new cabinet, headed by Laborite Einar Gerhardsen, who was destined to play a leading part in Norway's political life over the next quarter-century. The first postwar parliamentary election, in October 1945, gave Labor a clear majority and led to a new Gerhardsen-led cabinet.

## Sweden

Sweden was more fortunate than her neighbors: she was allowed to remain neutral throughout the war. She escaped the holocaust because neither the Soviet Union nor Hitler's Germany attacked her. Sweden was, therefore, not forced to accept the verdict of circumstances as were her neighbors. The goals of the larger powers, as events were to show, did not necessitate military action against Sweden. Sweden, for her part, did not consider Soviet aggression against Finland, or German subjugation of Denmark and Norway, as a sufficiently great threat to her own security to call for military action. The problem was, basically, the one the United States faced before Pearl Harbor defined, with all possible clarity, the enemy that had to be fought no matter what the cost. Sweden was spared a Pearl Harbor and was therefore able to cling to her neutrality.

By June 1940, with the occupation of Denmark and Norway, the dramatic collapse of Holland and Belgium, the amazingly speedy defeat of France, and the withdrawal of British forces from the Continent, Hitler's Germany appeared invincible and capable of imposing its will upon neutrals and belligerents alike.

Under these circumstances Sweden's neutrality policy was neither easy early in the war nor free from dangers in its later stages. The invasion of Denmark and Norway placed especially severe strains on Sweden's neutrality. When Germany informed Sweden, on April 9th, of the action in Denmark and Norway, the notification was accompanied by a demand for "complete" Swedish neutrality. The reply to the demand was that Sweden would continue neutral but that she reserved to herself the right "to adopt such measures" as might become necessary "to maintain and defend" her neutrality. Germany gave assurances that Sweden's stand and policy would be respected.

The assurances were repeatedly forgotten. In April, before Norwegian resistance to the German invasion had ended, Sweden was forced to agree to the transit of food and hospital supplies to the German forces in northern Norway. In June, after all of Norway had been occupied and France had capitulated, Sweden gave the Germans permission to transport military personnel to and from Norway (with the proviso that the transports would not increase the number of German forces in Norway). Other concessions were also made that aroused criticism in some quarters at the time but are fully understandable in retrospect. Perhaps outstanding among them was the permission, granted in June 1941, to transport a German division from Norway through Sweden to northern Finland. By the summer of 1943, however, all transit traffic through Sweden was ended and the export of certain important commodities to Germany had ceased; by the end of the year, Swedish-German commercial exchange had been reduced to a minimum. Meanwhile, generous aid to tens of thousands of Danish, Norwegian, and Finnish refugees had been provided—among them, thousands of Jews from Denmark who no doubt would otherwise have perished. The material aid given to Norway and Finland was of immense importance. For instance, it played a decisive part in enabling the hard-pressed Finns to overcome the economic paralysis caused by the war and the crippling reparations burden after 1944. If Sweden had been ravaged by war as her sister nations had been, all would have undoubtedly suffered a fate worse than that recorded during and after those tragic years.

SEVEN

POSTWAR ECONOMIC PATTERNS

## The Nature of the National Economies

The Scandinavian nations have free economies, in the usual sense of the term; this does not mean, however, that economic planning is nonexistent or of minor importance.

The term *planned economy* has often been used in a confusing manner in descriptions or analyses of the Scandinavian societies. The fact is, of course, that their economic development—no less than that of other countries—has involved planning in both the private and public sectors. This was true long before the twentieth century. The growth and expansion of private industry and the multiplicity of economic purposes and activities outlined in the annual budget of a modern nation clearly involve planning. The word *planning* and the concept it represents are obviously part of any meaningful definition of *economic activity*, whether private or public.

This is especially true of the World War II years and of much of the postwar period. During the war, all the Scandinavian countries were forced to abandon a number of pre-1939 policies and objectives and to substitute radically different wartime measures: rationing, price and foreign-exchange controls, import-export restrictions, programs for allocation of raw materials and labor, direction of defense and other industrial activity, and the like. All this involved planning to an exceptional degree and increased centralization and expansion of the concerns of the national governments. The end of the war reversed the trend: the reduction or dismantling of the huge wartime governmental and administrative apparatus became one of the major problems of the post-1945 years. But even after 1945, state authority— to provide and maintain the fullest possible employment, to build much-needed housing, to establish or expand ambitious social security

programs and related legislation, to revive vital foreign-trade opportunities—involved extensive planning.

The wartime and postwar economic policies of the Northern states
revealed a common characteristic: in many—if not most—instances,
government action meant emergency measures intended to deal with
crisis situations. State intervention in crisis situations was by no means
a new experience. It had existed on a fairly substantial scale during
World War I, and had become more conspicuous and elaborate during the depression years after 1929. With industry grinding to a
standstill, agriculture suffering from increasing paralysis, and the
country plagued by growing unemployment, it became impossible
for the state to remain a merely passive observer of the consequences
of economic stagnation. The various devices used during the 1930s in
the effort to achieve economic stability—for instance, Sweden's considerable use of government spending and Finland's policy underscor-
ing strict economy, both policies ultimately proving successful in overcoming the depression—left a record of "planned economy" upon
which governments could draw after 1939 in facing the complex
problems created by the war.

In dealing with these problems, the Scandinavian peoples have
drawn no clear line between state planning and free individual enterprise. The reason is, partly, that postwar reconstruction differed in
the four countries. Sweden, less affected by the war than Finland,
Denmark, or Norway, was able after 1945 to draw upon larger material resources and to recapture economic opportunities in foreign
markets more quickly than her sister democracies. Norway and Denmark, forced during the war to pay the costs of German occupation
and to finance extensive military installations—to say nothing of the
problem of restoring the property destroyed during the occupation—
faced intensified economic difficulties after the war. Finland, successful in escaping Soviet occupation, had to pay huge reparations to the
Soviet Union for eight long years (1944-52) during which the possibility of default—and the Soviet occupation which would have followed—were an ever-present threat. The volume and nature of the
reparations were such as to make unavoidable continuous and far-
reaching state participation and control of reparations industries. The
"normal" economy of the nation during these years was also subordinated, in many respects, to the requirements of the reparations
schedules and therefore reflected in a number of ways the continued
state direction.

It has been held that, since 1945, the Scandinavian countries have followed the policy of the "middle way" devised by Sweden in dealing with her economic problems in the 1930s. It is also maintained that this is the secret of their success in contending with pressing economic and social problems during the past twenty years. The fact is that, as a distinguished Danish observer has put it, the words "the policy of the 'middle way' are, literally, vague and uninformative."

The realities involved may be suggested by saying that the complexities of modern economy, especially on the international level, greatly increased by post-1939 developments, have made the production and distribution of Scandinavian commodities more vulnerable to circumstances outside the Scandinavians' control. The years since 1945 have called for greater economic adaptability to new and changing circumstances. In trying to promote permanent employment and the effective use of the means of production, in attempting to minimize or avoid market crises, and in raising national income to higher levels, the Scandinavian states have stepped forth to restrict and direct in order "to insure the best possible facilities for the free practice of economic activity." [1] The question of the extent of state intervention in the economy is, to a large degree, under continuing discussion; it is not readily answered on the basis of abstract conceptions regarding the "harmfulness" of private enterprise and the "advantages" of public enterprise.

The realities also include the fact that the past experience of these countries has led them to accept broad-fronted social legislation as one of the essentials of national welfare. The scale of this legislation justifies the term *social welfare state*. Also, there has long been in Scandinavia general acceptance (even among the conservative groups and parties) of state or municipal ownership and management of certain public utilities, such as railroads, gas and water works, electricity, certain telephone services, hospitals, harbor facilities and installations, and the like. It is a significant fact, incidentally, that nearly all public services were either established by or transferred from private ownership and control decades before the socialist parties had become important enough to command significant parliamentary strength. In other words, public ownership in various areas was originally carried through by conservatives and liberals who did not subscribe to the Marxist notion that "capitalist" institutions must be overthrown in order that a "better" society can be created.

[1] Thorkil Kristensen, in J. A. Lauwerys (ed.), *Scandinavian Democracy* (Copenhagen: J. H. Schultz, 1958), pp. 200, 203.

The public services have been and are mostly public utility monopolies. They are run according to approved business practices. The same applies also to some categories of the defense industries, part of the hydroelectric plants (in Norway, for instance, the state owns about one fourth of the power stations, while only about one third are privately owned), and certain mining and other industrial establishments.

Socialist ideology and programs—in Scandinavia as elsewhere—once called for the nationalization of the means of production in order to eliminate capitalistically organized private industry and to replace it by a noncapitalist economy producing (as the saying often went) for use and not for profit. This is no longer the case. Except for the Communists, who are not strong enough to impose their will on Scandinavian electorates or governments, the other leftist political parties do not advocate the nationalization of private industry. Party programs offer differing conceptions regarding what should be controlled and to what extent, how and when and how far restrictions, subsidies, or tax devices should be used in order to maintain production, distribution, employment, prices, and wages at satisfactory levels. The answers to these and related questions vary from country to country and with the passage of time. The goal of full employment in a free society remains a major political concern of political parties, legislative assemblies, and the council chambers of ministers of state, but it is no longer anchored to the inflexible ideology furnished by Marxist spokesmen as recently as two generations ago.

The economies of the Scandinavian lands are free economies—despite the fact that state-owned and state-directed economic enterprise, the economic activities of municipal or governmental authorities, and the role of the cooperatives are of considerable dimensions and have led some commentators to speak of "controlled capitalism" as a conspicuous characteristic of these nations. Sweden has frequently been singled out as an illustration of an economic structure in which capitalism is allegedly controlled in the interests of the "social welfare state."

Such interpretations miss the mark. A few basic facts regarding Sweden's economy more than suffice to underline the essentials involved. Approximately 94 per cent of the total industrial labor force of the nation is employed in private, free, competitive enterprise. Public-owned companies—ranging from railroads to certain defense industries—account for 6 per cent of the labor force. If one includes the employees of the cooperatives, themselves representatives of a highly competitive aspect of the nation's economy, and by no means "public" corporations in the ordinary sense of the term, the private industries' payrolls still account for 90 per cent of industrial workers.

Now it might be contended that, although there is an obvious distinction to be made between the planned economy of the Soviet Union and the Swedish system of economic control (as some have called it), the latter represents an economic order that differs sharply enough from the free-enterprise system to call for the designation *mixed-enterprise economy*. This designation might well be applied to Sweden and to the rest of Scandinavia. It is likely, however, to confuse rather than clarify unless one keeps in mind that it is relevant, broadly speaking, only to the extent to which it may be applied to the progressive Western democracies in general.

A controlled economy is one operated by a public authority that can set targets, plan and directly engage in production, decide priorities in the use of raw materials and in the allocation of the labor force, and control wages, savings, investments, exports and imports, the domestic retail trade, the essentials of agricultural production, and so on. Such a public authority—the state, in other words—and the economy it directs comprise a system that restricts the right of labor freely to move, organize, bargain, and strike in the pursuit of its objectives. And such a system inevitably leads to a contraction of the individual's general civil rights and liberties. The individual's choices and rights are limited or nonexistent; the state's *acta et dicta* furnish the decisive imperatives that bind one and all.

Merely to note these aspects and characteristics of controlled economies more than suffices to make it clear that the Scandinavian nations do not fit into this category. This basic fact is spelled out not only by the history of their economic development but by the past record and present functioning of their political and social institutions. (See Chapters Four and Five.)

### The Cooperatives

For well over two generations, the Scandinavians have demonstrated conspicuous success in establishing and developing a large variety of cooperative enterprises. The cooperative movement, intertwined with the social program, is part of the Scandinavian concept of "functioning social democracy." Such characterizations obscure the fact that the cooperatives are private businesses owned by large numbers of consumer-owners. Although the goal of the cooperatives is savings for the consumer and not profits for ownership and management (the distinction between savings and profits has been debated for years), their success depends upon principles and practices normally associated with private enterprise. That they have been successful is shown by the fact that the cooperatives have long been a firmly established sector of the Scandinavian economic structure, and that they have been lately expanding into many new areas.

The first cooperatives were consumers' or farmers' organizations. In recent decades, however, banking or credit institutions, insurance companies, manufacturing organizations, food-processing plants, dairies, bakeries, restaurants, flour mills, farms, breweries, publishing houses, housing enterprises, joint-purchasing organizations, and export and import organizations (to mention only a few) have become part of the cooperative structure. The structure also includes international aspects. As long ago as 1918 Denmark, Finland, Norway, and Sweden founded a joint importing corporation, with offices in Copenhagen and London; in 1939, they established the International Trading Agency, with headquarters in London.

One question has often been raised: What are the reasons for the success of the cooperative movement in the North? The question cannot be fully answered, because many intangibles are undoubtedly involved. It seems, however, that three basic factors were especially important. The first was economic need. The general standard of living was (at best) modest when the cooperatives first took hold. A commentator on the success of the Danish dairy cooperatives has described the situation in words that apply to the Scandinavian cooperative movement in general. The Danish cooperatives in the dairy field were born, she said, "out of sheer economic necessity," not out of idealistic considerations, and "these producers' cooperatives showed clearly the enormous value of joint economic effort."[2] The accumulation of savings, even small savings, was important in the economy of the anonymous Everyman. The cooperatives provided savings—in the consumer cooperatives, the savings were especially conspicuous rewards because they were distributed (usually once a year) on the basis of purchases made. It is difficult to see how the cooperatives could have been started and successfully developed in a more affluent society in which the need for saving pennies was not so urgent.

Another significant factor was the relatively high level of education

[2] Edith J. Hirsch, in Henning Friis, *Scandinavia Between East and West* (Ithaca, N.Y.: Cornell University Press, 1950), p. 202.

of the farmers and other citizens to whom the advocates of the cooperative idea addressed their appeal. The history of the movement appears to prove that the ability to understand and be persuaded, and the fact that the common people were able to provide from their own ranks individuals capable of comprehending their needs and the message urged by the friends of the cooperative idea, was a precondition for the success the cooperatives ultimately recorded.

Not less significant was the fact that the cooperative movement received much of its original stimulus from a small number of public-minded middle- and upper-class individuals who saw in it an aid in the effort to improve the conditions under which many of their fellow citizens lived. Dean Hans Christian Sonne, who started the first Scandinavian consumer cooperative in Denmark in 1866 and furnished the basic pattern for later cooperatives, was a splendid representative of this group. Professor Hannes Gebhard, who successfully launched the cooperative movement in Finland in 1899, was another who also saw in it a powerful aid in the general educational as well as economic advance of the Finns. In Sweden, university professors, journalists, and other intellectual leaders were directly or indirectly involved in the establishment of a number of cooperative societies in the 1890s, but it was an agricultural engineer—E. H. von Koch—who became responsible for the national cooperative movement in the country. A member of one of Sweden's leading families, actively interested in social reform, von Koch aided in the establishment of the Federation of Cooperatives in 1899, and served as its first General Secretary. The K.F. (Kooperativa Förbundet) became a propaganda and educational center serving the cause of the cooperatives. Consumers' cooperatives thereupon began to grow in a manner few could have foreseen in the early days of the movement. In Norway, similar leadership played a part in introducing the cooperatives and in securing their success.

It is thus clear that the cooperatives did not appear primarily as the result of the labors of the poorer citizens whose interests they were designed to serve; rather, they emerged under the auspices and leadership of exceptional individuals without whose endeavors the movement would have come a good deal later (if at all) and, possibly, with much smaller chances for success. Once the movement had taken hold, it became an integral part of the economy of the Scandinavian people.

The cooperative movement has illustrated, from the early days of

its history, the principle of self-government. Members have an equal
voice at general meetings of the cooperative societies; the amount of
annual purchases is not decisive. Membership is open to all. Profits
(i.e., "savings") are distributed among members on the basis of their
purchases at the cooperative. This system readily invites the conclusion that the cooperators practice an economic democracy unmarred
by the social and political distinctions discernible in many other areas
of national life. Certainly the local cooperative societies illustrate a
broadly based self-government; district and provincial associations
and national federations disclose the same democratic features.

Although the cooperatives are important in many areas of economic activity, they represent only a relatively small part of the total
economic concerns of the nations of the North. Their significance
varies from country to country, although approximately 40-50 per
cent of the citizenry of each nation are members of one or more cooperatives. Denmark illustrates the general trend in Scandinavia.
In 1912, agricultural products accounted for about 88 per cent of
Denmark's exports; in 1959, the figure was only 48 per cent. Slightly
more than half the exports thus consisted of industrial and other
nonagricultural commodities. Cooperatives account for some 80-90
per cent of the total production and sale of farm products, but consumer cooperatives—that is, retail shops—handle only about 10-12
per cent of the total retail trade.

In Finland, Norway, and Sweden the farmer produces primarily
for the domestic market. Most of the export commodities (80 per cent
or over) are paper, pulp, and a variety of other products derived from
lumber, iron ore, and the metal and engineering industries. Certain
differences have also appeared in the retail trade. Finnish cooperatives, for instance, have outdistanced those of their Northern neighbors by a substantial margin: about 30 per cent of the retail trade is
accounted for by the cooperatives. In Sweden the corresponding
figure appears to be about 10-12 per cent; in Norway, somewhat less.
The rate of expansion or growth of the cooperatives during the past
two or three decades suggests that these figures and proportions are
not likely to change very much in the future and that the movement
may have entered a leveling-off stage.

The notable success of the cooperative movement in Scandinavia
has obviously depended upon many factors. Outstanding among them
is, as has been suggested, the relatively high educational level of the
member groups. The so-called folk high schools have played a par-

ticularly prominent role (especially since the turn of the century) in changing the common folk into a citizenry sufficiently wide awake and well informed to see the advantages of the cooperative movement. In the words of Anders Nielsen, a leading figure in the Danish cooperative movement:

> . . . we must acknowledge with gratitude the great religious and school leaders Grundtvig and Kold . . . who called forth a higher culture and feeling of solidarity among the people, and who taught the people to think and use their capacities so as to develop their lives in such a way that the united efforts of all insure that not only the individual but the whole community is benefited.[3]

N. F. S. Grundtvig (1783-1872) was a clergyman, poet, and historian; Kristen Kold (1816-1870) was an educator. Bishop Grundtvig founded the Danish folk high schools; Kold provided the pattern for the successful forms of this interesting scheme of adult education. Grundtvig urged, after 1836, that adults should be provided with special education, concentrating on "the national and community life we all can and must share in." He was a strong nationalist, eager to aid the Danish cause in predominantly German Schleswig, and it was in northern Schleswig that the first folk high school was founded in 1844. The movement began to gain ground, however, only after Kold opened his school in northwest Jutland, at Ryslinge, in 1851. Other folk high schools soon appeared in many parts of the country. They appealed primarily to farmers, who attended them in growing numbers. The schools therefore played an important part in raising the farmers' educational level and in stimulating their interest in local and national problems. Before long, many of the former students of the schools were found among the leaders of the cooperative movement, various progressive political activities, and other socially important endeavors.

By the close of the 1870s, the Danish folk high schools were rapidly increasing in number. By the end of the century, they exercised a strong influence upon the nation and had also become a part of the educational system of the other Northern lands. The schools have

---

[3] Quoted in F. C. Howe in *Denmark, A Cooperative Commonwealth* (New York: Coward-McCann, Inc., 1925), p. 49. I have offered a summary of the importance of the folk high schools in Vol. II, Chapter 13 of R. E. Tugwell and Leon Keyserling (eds.), *Redirecting Education* (New York: Columbia University Press, 1935).

never become large: few of them have over one hundred students. Annual enrollment does not normally exceed 7000-7500 in Denmark and in Sweden, 4000 in Finland, and 5800 in Norway. Although the schools have undergone considerable change during the past generation, they have continued to serve as significant centers of adult education.[4]

## Agriculture

Scandinavia is, obviously, a geographically peripheral part of Europe. In an economic sense, the Scandinavians remained on the periphery of industrialized Europe until past the middle of the nineteenth century. Since that time, however, the picture has radically changed. Industrialization, relatively slow at first, but proceeding with increasing speed, has contributed more than anything else during the past seventy-five years toward making the four Scandinavian nations what they are today. Urbanization, the mode of living in town and country alike, the composition and shape of the population pyramid, the movement of persons and goods from place to place, foods, eating and drinking habits, the manner of dress, the press, and much of the Scandinavians' conception of the world and of the universe— all reflect and illustrate the impact of industrialization, and the magnitude of the revolution it has wrought in these northern latitudes.

One of the most striking measures of the transformation caused by industrialization is the change in agriculture. The change is, broadly speaking, two-fold: First, agriculture has become mechanized and scientific; farming has become a vocation that the great-grandfather of today's farmer would hardly recognize. Second, in the preponderantly non-agrarian economies of the nations of the North, agriculture no longer occupies most of the national labor force, and its products are no longer able to compete, in terms of money value, with the contributions to national income of industry, trade, commerce, shipping, and other nonagricultural categories of economic activity. This is as true of Denmark, where about 75 per cent of the area of the country is under cultivation, as it is of Finland (9-10 per cent), Norway (3 per cent), and Sweden (9-10 per cent).

[4] The observance of the centenary of the first Norwegian folk high school, August 15-16, 1964, offered one of many illustrations of the importance of these schools. King Olav attended a jubilee service, a part of the observance program; a distinguished scholar, Professor Sigmund Skard, delivered the main address; and 300 educators from Denmark, Finland, Sweden and Norway attended a conference arranged for the occasion.

The role of agriculture in Finland's economy before 1939 was determined, to a considerable degree, by the land-reform legislation passed between 1918 and the mid-1930s.

For about a generation before World War I, the growing problem of the landless rural population had made it clear that a satisfactory solution had to be found. Unless a remedy for the plight of the landless was devised, mounting social, political, and economic difficulties would beset the nation. In 1901, about one third of the rural families were tenant farmers; about 18 per cent could be said to have no home of their own; over 40 per cent owned no land except small garden plots. Many of the tenant farmers held short-term leases. Finland thus began the twentieth century burdened with a pressing agrarian problem. A few inadequate measures were enacted before 1917, but it was not until the country had become independent that a genuine reform was carried through.

The first agrarian law was passed in October 1918, some ten months after the declaration of independence; other laws followed in 1921 and 1922. The results of this legislation were impressive. Between 1919 and 1935, about 117,000 new holdings, owned by former tenants, were created. The improvement of the lot of the tenant farmer did not, however, eliminate the problem; it was still necessary to make it possible for individuals desirous of becoming independent farmers to obtain land on reasonable terms. The problem was solved in 1922 by a law providing land for settlement. Its purpose was to provide state funds for land purchases, at moderate rates of interest. The law also fixed the price of land at the 1914 level, and the maximum acreage the prospective farmer could buy. The State financed the whole transaction, if necessary; no down payment was required. If no state-owned or municipal land was available, individual owners could be forced to sell a certain percentage of their acreage if they owned more than 500 acres and if the land was not considered efficiently farmed.

As a result of these reform measures, new independent owners acquired 3.56 million acres of land previously owned by private individuals or corporations and 779,000 acres of state-owned land. By 1937, nearly nine tenths of the farms were held by independent owners, and tenancy had nearly disappeared. By the end of 1934, all but $750,000 of the loans advanced by the state had been repaid. The huge reform had been carried through by voluntary sale and purchase; litigation, allowed by law, appears to have been involved in only one instance. The degree to which the small farmer dominates the scene in Finland is suggested by the fact that, in 1950, only 223 out of a total of 356,786 farms had more than 250 acres.

Danish land problems and reform measures differed from the Finnish in several respects. The Danish peasant had lived under virtually feudal conditions until the closing decades of the eighteenth century. The next half-century witnessed many changes for the better: by the middle of the nineteenth century, nearly two thirds of the Danish farms were freehold properties. After 1860, factors beyond the Danes' control threatened the very basis of the nation's agrarian economy. The coming of the railroad and the steamship made it possible for other nations to transport and sell grain in Europe at prices ruinous to Danish farmers. The effort to find a way out of the difficulty resulted in a radical change of the agricultural system of the country: traditional grain-growing was abandoned and large-scale animal husbandry was introduced. The agricultural schools and the cooperatives played a leading part in affecting the change from the old economic structure to the new.

The attempt to stimulate intensive livestock farming included efforts to increase the number of small or medium-sized holdings owned by independent farmers. A law enacted in 1899 offered state loans covering 90 per cent of the cost of small farm properties. During the next two decades, about 9300 new holdings were established. Additional measures after World War I provided funds for further small land-holder loans and, by 1932, some 6200 new farms had been created. Approximately 21,000 owners of holdings have been enabled to acquire additional acreage by means of government support. According to a government publication of 1961,[5] the total number of Danish farms is about 200,000, nearly half of which (93,000) are less than twenty-five acres in size; only 865 have more than 300 acres. Tenancy, not as serious a problem in Denmark as it was in Finland before 1918, had nearly vanished. Since 1938, the government has also offered loans on easy terms to agricultural laborers for home construction. Denmark conforms in all respects to the agricultural world of the North: it is a world of the small farmer whose income and standard of living have registered great improvement, especially during the past two generations.

The importance of agriculture in the North is not measured only by land ownership, the absence of tenancy, or the dominant position

[5] The Royal Danish Ministry of Foreign Affairs, *Denmark* (Copenhagen: 1961), pp. 444-45.

of the small farmer; other factors of great importance are involved. Among them is the fact that, although agriculture is—by a substantial margin—the largest Danish export industry (about 60 per cent of the agricultural production is for export), its products are intended primarily for the domestic market in Finland, Norway, and Sweden. But even in Denmark the role of the farmer in foreign trade has significantly changed. In 1912, about 88 per cent of Denmark's exports consisted of agricultural commodities, such as cattle, pigs, bacon, butter, cheese, eggs, and the like. By 1937, this figure had declined to 71 per cent; by 1959, to 48 per cent. Industrial exports, on the other hand, had risen from 12 per cent in 1912 to 45 per cent in 1959. Denmark has thus ceased to be a country specializing almost exclusively in agricultural production. The change in export patterns has been matched by corresponding changes in the import structure. Cereals, feeds, and fertilizers accounted for nearly 30 per cent of the imports in 1912, but only a little over 10 per cent in 1959; machinery and related products, which had accounted for only one per cent in 1912, had risen to 12 per cent by 1959.

In Finland, Norway, and Sweden, agriculture—although important —plays a subordinate part in foreign trade. In 1962, for example, agricultural products accounted for only 4 per cent of Finland's exports. The figure for Norway was about the same in 1959, and that for Sweden only slightly higher. The general basis of the economy of these three countries is not agriculture but the riches of their forests, mines, waterfalls, and seas.

The situation of the small farmer is basically the same in Norway as it is in Sweden. Norway is overwhelmingly a nation of small landholders. Over 90 per cent of the farms have less than twenty-five acres of arable land; in 1959, only forty-three holdings could boast of 250 acres or more. The mountainous nature of the country and the great number of fjords account for the fact that only 3 per cent of the area is under cultivation—and this, in turn, explains why by far the greater part of wheat and rye must be imported. Norway's own production of breadstuffs comes to only 10 per cent of the country's needs.

A similar situation prevails in Sweden. Out of about 300,000 farms, only some 8000 have 125 acres or more. Because of the size of the country and its population, and the availability of relatively large areas of good farmland in the southern provinces, agricultural production and self-sufficiency reach higher levels in Sweden than in Norway. Sweden's wheat production, for example, meets her domestic needs, as does her production of sugar beet and some other com-modities.

The marked decline in the importance of agriculture has been shown, among other things, by the decreasing proportion of the population dependent upon farming and forestry (the two are often combined in Scandinavian statistics) as a main source of income. To-day only some 20-26 per cent of the Scandinavian population belongs in this category. Even Denmark's agriculture accounts for only about 26 per cent of the population; in Finland—where only two or three decades ago, some two thirds of the population was agrarian—the figure is 25-26 per cent; and the figure is lower still for Sweden and Norway. Farming has thus ceased to be the major economic activity in Scandinavia. Despite this fact, a greater national self-sufficiency in food has become a fact since World War I.

Much of the greater self-sufficiency in food is, however, more seem-ing than real. Production levels have been driven upward by a greater dependence on machines, fuels, lubricants, fertilizers, feeds, and other commodities largely or partly imported from abroad. Thus the increased self-sufficiency in food has been reached, in considerable degree, only by increasing dependence upon foreign sources. World War II demonstrated this fact in a manner that will not soon be for-gotten. Any major future war will, at the very least, repeat the demon-stration and again underline the mutual dependence inherent in the international division of labor and services that make international trade possible.

*Industry*

The decline of the relative importance of agriculture in Scandi-navia, in view of the area's notable general economic advance, im-plies that the Northern countries have become large-scale producers of other commodities. Such is indeed the case: industry has not only become important in the Scandinavian economy but, in some re-spects, dominates the scene.

Denmark provides a particularly vivid illustration of the impact of industrialization on Scandinavia. Denmark lacks nearly all basic natural resources: most raw materials must be imported: cotton, wool, rubber, iron and other metals, timber and wood products in general, and practically all fuels come from abroad. Yet manufacturing indus-tries in Denmark have grown at a rapid pace and today make a larger contribution to the national economy than any other category of eco-nomic activity. The significant beginnings of industrialization, after

1870, were connected with the reorganization of agricultural production from grain-growing to dairy farming. During the past generation, and especially since World War II, industrial growth—both in volume and in diversity—has been marked. Between 1935 and 1959, industrial output nearly doubled, as did the export of industrial commodities. In 1960, industry employed 285,000 workers—85,000 of them were women—in about 6000 industrial establishments, about a score of which employed over 1000 workers each.

Not the least notable aspect of Denmark's industrial pattern is the fact that in 1959 the metals, ship-building, and engineering industries employed over 100,000 workers—approximately two fifths of the total industrial labor force—and accounted for one third of the value of the nation's industrial output. The production of ships, chemicals, plastics, machinery, beverages, food preserves, high-grade textiles, silver, tableware, furniture, and scores of other products testifies to the variety and volume of Danish enterprise in the industrial field. About 25 per cent of the total output of manufactured goods is exported, mostly to European countries. Britain and West Germany are Denmark's best customers.

The industrial sector of Finland's economy had steadily expanded, especially during the interwar years. World War II severely restricted some industries, paralyzed others (the textile industry, for example), and greatly stimulated still others, among them those engaged in the production of munitions and war materials. After the 1944 armistice, the nation faced two immense difficulties: one, the severe depletion of the nation's basic industrial resource—the forests—as a result of territorial cessions to the Soviet Union; the other, the huge reparations bill that had to be met lest the country expose itself to the possibility of Soviet occupation. Reparations payments placed tremendous demands upon the industrial capacity of the Finns, for they meant, obviously, exports for which no equivalent would come from the Soviet Union.

Once the enormous reparations payments had been completed, it was discovered that they actually provided a substantial long-range economic advantage. By 1953, the industries involved in providing reparations goods—especially the ship-building, metals, and machinery industries—had been greatly modernized, expanded, and raised to levels of high-quality production largely unknown before 1939. The onerous reparations years also yielded an accumulation of technical know-how and managerial experience unattainable during the years before the war.

These and related factors explain Finland's post-1945 industrial expansion, which is unmatched in the history of the country. In 1962, the total industrial production was over 300 per cent that of 1938, and about 400 per cent that of 1944; in metals, the growth over 1938 was 471 per cent; in chemicals, 796 per cent; in mining, 415 per cent. In such "old" industries as wood, paper, textiles, and food-processing, 1962 production figures were from 50 per cent to nearly 400 per cent higher than those for 1938. The industrial labor force had grown from 220,000 in 1937 to 415,000 in 1961.

Norway is no exception to the Scandinavian pattern of industrialization. In 1865, approximately 16 per cent of the population was employed in industrial establishments (most of which were small). By the turn of the century, the figure had grown to 26 per cent and gradually rose thereafter; in 1950, slightly over one third of the labor force was employed in industrial establishments. Industrial products, which accounted for only 10 per cent of Norway's annual exports in the late 1870s, had risen to about 33 per cent by the early years of the twentieth century.

World War II delivered a severe blow to Norway's industry. Parts of it virtually ceased to operate, not the least because of the ruthless exactions of the Germans. During 1940-45, nearly one third of the total industrial assets of the country were lost, and general production was reduced to about half that of prewar periods. Inevitably, the industries producing for export suffered most, but no important sector of Norway's industry escaped the blight of the war years.

Recovery since 1945 has been steady and, relatively, of the same magnitude as elsewhere in Scandinavia. By the late 1950s, the annual volume of industrial production was almost three times as great as that reached in the late 1930s. The iron, metals, and food-processing industries had become the largest employers of labor, followed by pulp, paper, textiles, and chemical plants. The country's flourishing export industries—resting especially on her forests, mineral resources, and the utilization of large water-power resources—today account for some 20 per cent of the workers in industry and about one quarter of the total industrial production. Paper and paper board, basic metals, raw materials, fish and fish products, pulp, and machinery head the list of export commodities. Both exports and imports were valued, in 1959, at a figure nearly four times larger than that for 1939.

Fishing, whaling, and shipping have long been leading aspects of Norway's economy. About 60,000-70,000 persons are employed in the fishing industry. Although the average annual catch in the early 1920s was 500,000-600,000 tons, it had grown to well over 1 million tons by the late 1950s. Dried, salted, fresh, frozen, and canned fish were the fourth largest category of export commodities in 1959.

Modern whaling, especially before 1939, was in considerable degree a business dominated by the Norwegians. This was natural, in view of the fact that the basic modern whaling techniques were invented by Norwegians: the grenade harpoon fired from motor-driven whale-boats in the 1860s, the "floating factory" first used in the Antarctic in 1905, and the ship equipped with a slipway in the stern, permitting the hauling aboard of the whale for processing, in 1925. Before 1939, Norway's share in whale oil production was about 50 per cent; Great Britain, Argentina, Japan, and Germany accounted for the rest. The industry suffered heavy losses during World War II. The years since 1945 have witnessed a relative decline in Norwegian whaling and the emergence of Japan and the Soviet Union as leading competitors. Japan in particular has expanded her whaling activities; cheap labor and the fact that the Japanese eat whale meat while Westerners as a rule do not, account for much of the advantage enjoyed by the Japanese.

Norway's economy, with its diversified modern industry and dependence on foreign trade, could not have produced the high standard of living the Norwegians have long enjoyed were it not for the all-important shipping industry. On the eve of World War II, the Norwegian merchant fleet of 4.8 million gross tons was the fourth-largest in the world. The merchant fleet served the Allied cause during the war and suffered severe losses: the tonnage had been reduced to 2.7 million when the war ended.

The rebuilding and expansion of the fleet since 1945 has been very rapid. By the summer of 1950, the tonnage afloat totaled 5.1 million, considerably more than that of 1939. Although most of the building contracts had to be placed abroad—in 1959, for instance, ships accounted for 22 per cent of the country's imports—the effort was carried forward with speed and despatch: the 8 million-ton mark had been passed by 1957, and on January 1, 1961, Norway's merchant fleet came to 11.2 million gross tons—about 8.5 per cent of the total world tonnage.

The main importance of Norwegian shipping, in the larger context of the nation's economy, lies in its foreign-currency earnings, which are vital to the maintenance of the high level of Norway's imports. Norway herself does not produce enough to furnish full equivalents for the imports the country's high standard of living requires. The balance—some 75 per cent—is made up by the earnings of the merchant fleet.

Sweden is, by a substantial margin, the leading industrial nation of the North. The bases of her pre-eminence are large forest resources, extensive deposits of unusually pure iron ore, and abundant water power. To these indispensables are added the industrial skills and techniques accumulated over many generations, especially in the metals and engineering sectors of industry.

An indication of Sweden's industrial growth is provided by the fact that, although as recently as 1930 a majority of her population earned their living at agriculture, by 1962 only about 12 per cent of the "economically active population" were engaged in farming while the number employed in industry was three times as large.

Another measure of the importance of industry is suggested by the fact that, by the early 1960s, agriculture accounted for only 5 per cent of the country's gross national product. In 1960, the industrial labor force had grown to about 700,000. Metals, ship-building, and engineering industries accounted for by far the greater part of this figure—321,000 workers; wood, pulp, and paper industries, for 115,000; textiles and clothing industries, for 80,000; and chemicals, leather, and rubber industries, for 53,000.

Although Sweden is not in the front rank of European shipping nations, her merchant fleet is by no means negligible. Heavy losses during World War II were quickly recouped after 1945, and by 1963 the ocean-going fleet reached about 5.5 million tons, or some 3 per cent of the world total. Meantime, Sweden has also become a leading builder of ships. In 1962, for example, the tonnage launched by Swedish shipyards amounted to 860,000, or one tenth of the world output (Japan, Britain, and West Germany headed the list). Nearly three fourths of the ships were for foreign registry and thus represented an important item in the country's exports.

Sweden's domestic market is altogether unable to absorb more than a part of the produce of many of her industries. This is especially true of wood, paper, pulp, iron ore, and the metals and engineering industries. In recent years, certain products once wholly or almost wholly used at home have entered the category of export commodities —among them, readymade wearing apparel, furniture, and automobiles.

Most of Sweden's industrial exports go to European markets. This concentration on European markets is of long standing, but has grown lately. Today about 80 per cent of Swedish exports go to Europe. Denmark, Finland, and Norway alone absorbed 15.1 per cent of Swedish exports in 1953, and 23.2 per cent in 1963. West Germany, Sweden's best customer, took 11.5 per cent in 1953, and 14.2 per cent in 1963. Britain accounted for 19 per cent in 1953, and 13.5 per cent in 1963.

### Foreign Trade

It is abundantly clear that Scandinavia's industries have reached a stage where they produce a variety of commodities greatly in excess of the needs of the North. The Scandinavians therefore must exchange their excess production for the raw materials and commodities essential for their industries and general consumer needs. Thus foreign trade in substantial volume is a must for each of the four nations.

Before 1939, Germany was the main trading partner of the Northern nations. World War II changed the situation in several respects. First, a defeated, divided Germany could play only a minor part in the foreign trade of Scandinavia for some years after 1945. After the early 1950s, West Germany forged ahead rapidly and had become a major Scandinavian market ten years later. Second, the Soviet Union rose to new importance after the war. Soviet foreign trade with the North was negligible before 1939. Although the volume of Scandinavia's trade with the Soviet Union since 1945 has in no sense approached that of her trade with Britain or West Germany, it has increased by a substantial margin.

The greatest increase has been in Finnish-Soviet trade. Before 1939, Finland's exports to and imports from the Soviet Union amounted to 1-2 per cent of her total foreign trade. The huge reparations payments in 1945-52 changed the picture and led to a new economic relationship. Although Finland's foreign trade has remained overwhelmingly Western-oriented (approximately 80 per cent of her exports go to Western markets), the Soviet share has substantially increased since 1952. In 1958, 17.3 per cent of Finland's exports went to the Soviet Union; in 1960, 14.2 per cent; in 1961-64, 12-13 per cent. In the case of Denmark, each of the first ten of her trading partners absorbs larger quantities of Danish goods than does the Soviet Union; among them are the United States and Brazil in the Western Hemisphere, and the United Kingdom, West Germany, East Germany, Sweden, Norway, and Italy in Europe. Norway's export-import relationship with the Soviet Union is negligible (about 1.5 per cent of her total foreign trade), and the same is true of Sweden.

It has been contended that Finland's trade relations with the Soviet Union constitute a dangerous dependence on the Soviet market that

Moscow might use for political purposes. Soviet refusal to continue to buy from Finland, it has been claimed, would expose the republic to pressures destructive of its freedom. The metals and ship-building industries are, allegedly, particularly vulnerable because they produce, in considerable degree, for the Soviet market. It seems, however, that such interpretations lack solid foundation in fact. About 80 per cent of the products of the metals and machine industries, for example, are absorbed by the domestic market. Of the amount exported, the Soviets took about 70 per cent (the average for the years 1954-62); the other nations in the Eastern bloc, about 2-5 per cent. Also, there appears to be no reason for assuming that if considerations of economic advantage (hitherto decisive in determining Soviet purchases in Finland) were abandoned by the Soviets, Finland's economy could not cope with the difficulties presented by a 12-15 per cent loss of exports. Finally, the record of Finnish-Soviet trade relations since 1952 appears to justify the conclusion that Soviet observance of trade agreements with Finland has been, possibly because of prestige considerations, meticulously correct.[6]

The foreign-trade position of Denmark, Norway, and Sweden has, on the whole, remained unchanged as far as the East-West blocs are concerned. The Soviet Union and Eastern Europe have been of only secondary importance to Danish foreign trade since 1945. The sales to Britain, Denmark's best foreign customer, are approximately ten to eleven times larger than her combined exports to the Soviet Union and the satellite nations of Eastern Europe (the Soviets account for more than half this total). In Norway, the situation was much the same: in the late 1950s, the Soviet Union took only about 2 per cent of Norway's exports; the other Eastern-bloc countries, slightly over 0.5 per cent. The United Kingdom, on the other hand, absorbed somewhat over 20 per cent; West Germany, about 15 per cent; and the United States, approximately 10 per cent of Norway's exports. Denmark, Finland, and Sweden alone bought, in terms of money value,

[6] Percentages of exports and imports or other figures do not tell the whole story, to be sure. Foreign-exchange controls, subsidies, export premiums, import restrictions, and other measures common to the post-1945 commercial policies of many nations have created many difficulties in foreign trade. Finland's export-import relationship has meant, over the past many years, a twofold advantage. First, some Finnish products can be more advantageously sold in the Soviet Union than in the West. Second, although many commodities bought from the Soviets could also be obtained from the West, buying them from the Soviet Union (by paying for them with Finnish exports) frees Finland from certain foreign-exchange difficulties.

about eight times the amount of goods sold by Norway in the Soviet Union. Sweden's foreign trade was similarly oriented. Britain, West Germany, and the United States in particular accounted for by far the greater part of Sweden's products consumed abroad.[7]

[7] Scandinavia's dependence on foreign markets also means a marked degree of reciprocal dependence by her foreign-trade partners. In 1935, for example, 7.8 per cent of Britain's exports went to Scandinavia; 6.3 per cent, to the United States; 5.6 per cent to West Germany; and 4.9 per cent to France. Thus the North was easily Britain's best European customer. In Asia, India (with a population of 300 million as compared with Scandinavia's 20 million) absorbed 8 per cent of Britain's exports. Scandinavia remains a significant user of British products.

## General

Iceland is part of the Scandinavian group of nations. A history extending over a thousand years and language and national preferences that rest upon affinities of long standing make the island an integral part of the Northern culture area. In recent decades, Iceland has been a conspicuous and active partner in the expansion of Scandinavian cooperation. And the fact that Iceland's Scandinavian neighbors live a thousand miles to the east, beyond the waters of the Atlantic, has not prevented the Icelanders from developing political institutions and democratic processes basically similar to those described in Chapters Four and Five.

Iceland, with an area of 39,602 square miles, is slightly larger than Indiana, four times the size of Massachusetts, and about one tenth smaller than Virginia or Ohio. In Europe, Portugal is smaller by some 4000 square miles; Ireland (Eire) and North Ireland, combined, by nearly 7000 square miles; Belgium and the Netherlands, combined, by about 5000 square miles.

Iceland extends north to the Arctic Circle, and south to about 63°N. Despite the high latitude of the island, its climate is, thanks to the Gulf Stream, relatively mild. Nevertheless, it varies greatly. Somewhat over 5000 square miles (about 13 per cent of the total area) are covered by snowfields or glaciers. The climate in the interior is often very cold, while the coastal areas in the south and west enjoy an oceanic type of climate. In Reykjavik, the capital, the average July temperature is about 52°F.; the average January temperature, about 30°F.

Iceland, "Land of Ice and Fire," has a large number of hot springs, found in all parts of the country. They represent a unique national resource: the houses in the capital, and many others in the countryside, are heated by this natural hot water. Because of the hot water, greenhouses are able to grow tropical and other fruit. Iceland is also one of the most volcanic regions in the world, and many of the volcanoes have been active for centuries. Some of the eruptions have brought great destruction and disaster. In the 1780s, the outbreak of one of the volcanoes killed over half of the island's cattle, two thirds of the horses, and four fifths of the sheep. After the eruption, famine struck the land, claiming over 9000 lives—or one fifth of the total population. Earthquakes, although common, rarely cause extensive damage. A volcanic eruption in November 1963 created a new island off the southern coast.

A recent writer has given an excellent description of the country in general:

> . . . a unique and hauntingly beautiful landscape, . . . a mountainous land, with towering peaks and curious rock formations; in some ways it has the look of an unfinished world. . . . But everywhere there is abundant beauty, with huge lava fields alternating with glittering glaciers and green valleys, with rushing rivers, tumbling waterfalls and placid lakes.[1]

It is not only in terms of location and geography that Iceland differs greatly from the other Scandinavian lands; the island's population is only a fraction of that of the other lands of the North. Iceland had about 50,000 people in 1700, but the number had declined to 47,000 a century later. In 1900, the figure stood at 78,000; by 1952, it had reached 150,000; by 1962, 181,200. Iceland is thus one of the smallest nations in the world. Somewhat over 60 per cent of the population is urban. Reykjavik had 75,000 inhabitants in 1962, but most of the other cities had well under 5000.

Iceland was first settled as early as the ninth century; it was discovered by the Scandinavians about 850, although the land had already been partly inhabited by earlier settlers, some of them from the British Isles. For some four centuries, Iceland was an independent republic composed of a number of small, loosely united chieftaincies. The islanders set up a legislative assembly, the Althing, in 930, and thus became the founders of the oldest parliament in Europe. Christianity was introduced from Norway in the late 990s; the conversion of the Icelanders is usually dated from the year 1000—the date that marks the Althing's acceptance (after a good deal of fighting) of a

[1] Erik J. Friis, in *The American-Scandinavian Review* (June 1964), 159.

compromise decision regarding the old heathen religion and the new Christian creed. The decision was that the people of the island would be baptized and the temples of the old gods be destroyed; private sacrifice to the old gods would be allowed, but anyone making a public sacrifice would be outlawed. Heathen views and practices, however, did not disappear overnight; generations were to pass before Christianity was fully accepted.

## To Self-rule and Independence

Scandinavia in general and Iceland in particular reveal that the basic complexities of economic life, government, and politics usually associated with large, populous nations are also present in the small nations. The emergence of Iceland—first as an autonomous state and ultimately as an independent nation—illustrates the truth of this assertion.

Until well into the nineteenth century, Iceland remained under direct Danish rule. The economic life of the small nation was controlled by the Danes during most of the seventeenth and eighteenth centuries, and politically the island remained subordinated to Copenhagen, where (see pages 46-47) an absolute monarchy had emerged in 1660-65. The Althing was abolished in 1800, and although it was revived as a consultative assembly in 1843, Iceland's political and administrative status did not improve until after 1874.

The improvement came, in large degree, in response to the growing demand of Icelandic nationalists determined to obtain full recognition of their people as a separate national and political entity. Their first great success came in 1874, when Iceland was given a constitution of its own. The new fundamental law granted legislative power to the Althing and provided for Icelandic self-government in domestic affairs, including control of finances. Complete home rule was obtained in 1904, on the basis of a measure of Icelandic authorship. The next step leading to independence came in 1918, when the Danish-Icelandic Act of Union became law.

The Act of Union was a measure drawn up by Danish and Icelandic negotiators, approved by the legislatures of the two nations, and accepted by an overwhelming majority in a plebiscite in Iceland. Its main provision stated that Iceland and Denmark are "free sovereign states united by a common king." Denmark remained, for practical reasons, in charge of Iceland's foreign affairs, but she retained no control over Icelandic affairs, and was represented in Reykjavik by a minister plenipotentiary. The Act also provided that the agreement

could be ended, after 1940, if either the Danish or the Icelandic legislature demanded it; if a new treaty had not been concluded within
three years of the demand for termination, either legislature could
consider the Act as having lapsed.

The Act of 1918 and its implications took on an unexpected meaning in April 1940, when Denmark was occupied and the German subjugation of Norway began. On April 10th, concluding that the king
was no longer able to conduct Iceland's foreign affairs, the Althing
vested executive power in the cabinet. The cabinet thereupon voted
to end its allegiance to the Crown. On May 17th, the legislature declared that Iceland had the right to revoke the Act, appointed a regent to exercise supreme power, and announced that Iceland would
be established as a republic upon the formal dissolution of its union
with Denmark.

The Althing resolved, on February 25, 1944, to end the agreement.
A national plebiscite, in which 98 per cent of the adult citizens participated, confirmed the decision of the legislature on May 20-23,
1944: the vote was 71,122 for, 377 against. A republican constitution
was then voted by the Althing and accepted by a popular vote of
69,435 to 1051. On June 17, 1944, Iceland became a sovereign republic.

The constitutional changes carried through when World War I
began had established complete political democracy in Iceland.
Women as well as men had the unrestricted right to vote; the legislature was chosen directly by the people; and parliamentary government had been established in 1904. Freedom of the press, of assembly,
and of association, and other rights of the individual were secure. Although the Lutheran Church was the state church, freedom of conscience was guaranteed. These and related aspects of a functioning
democracy were carried over, needless to say, to the years after 1918
and have remained the solid foundations of life in Iceland.

The president is elected directly by the voters for a four-year term.
The functioning executive is the cabinet, normally composed of six
members. Coalition cabinets are the rule because of the multiparty
system that prevails. There are six parties, ranging from Conservatives
to Communists (the latter have been a permanent minority). The
Althing of fifty-two members is divided into an upper house of seventeen and a lower house of thirty-five members. All important bills
are introduced and decided in the united Althing.

World War II also changed Iceland's status and relations with foreign powers. For about eight months after the outbreak of the war in September 1939, Britain recognized Iceland's neutrality. On May 10, 1940, however, the British landed forces at Reykjavik and proceeded to occupy the country. (The action came a month after the Nazi invasion of Denmark and Norway and coincided with Hitler's attack upon the Low Countries and the invasion of France.) Britain's action was justified, London claimed, because it prevented the Germans from taking possession of the island. (There appears to be no doubt but that the Germans would have occupied Iceland and used it as a base against the Allies if they had not been forestalled by the British.)

It was made clear that the occupation was by a friendly power not intent on conquest. The British did not set up a puppet government and avoided interfering with Iceland's government, administration, or press. This did not suffice, however, to prevent all expressions of Icelandic displeasure over the presence of foreign troops. The troops numbered between 60,000 and 80,000 men—about half the population of the country.

The British forces were withdrawn toward the end of June 1941. At Britain's suggestion, Iceland thereupon invited the United States' troops to take over the island for the duration. An agreement providing for the American occupation was signed on July 8, 1941; some of the troops had landed on the preceding day. After the war had ended, the United States raised the question, in October 1945, of future bases on the island. The question was extensively discussed and debated in Iceland; the Communists in particular favored speedy and complete withdrawal of American forces. The question was finally settled on March 30, 1949, when Iceland joined NATO. Keflavik and its military installations (manned, according to unofficial reports, by some 4000-5000 Americans) remain the principal sign of Iceland's readiness to participate in the defense arrangements of the free West.

### The Economic Scene

Two generations ago, Iceland was but little developed. As one Icelander has put it:

> At the turn of the century, the Icelandic economy was much the same as it had been in medieval times. Cultivation of the soil with modern methods had hardly begun, fishing was done by hand line, Iceland did not own a single merchant vessel, there was no harbor, . . . there was hardly a bridge in the country, and only a few kilometers of road.

And this in a country the size of Denmark, the Netherlands and Belgium together. . . .[2]

There were practically no industries other than cottage or handicraft industries hardly worthy of the name.

Since the turn of the century, the picture has changed greatly. By 1914, Iceland was connected with the European continent by telegraph; Reykjavik had a harbor; a fleet of modern trawlers and motorized ships had been acquired; and growing exports had become a significant factor in the nation's life. Today, some 20 per cent of the people are employed in industry; about one third of the workers are women. Food-processing—fish, butter, meats, dried milk, confectionery, and so on—and textiles account for most of the nation's industries; cement, fertilizers, chemicals, and shoe manufacture have grown in importance. Most of the industrial establishments are located in or near Reykjavik. The reason for the change and the advance is, basically, that the Icelanders have succeeded in developing an important export industry that rests on the rich resources of the sea. "Iceland has been able to become large in a small field and then offset the disadvantage which the small size of the country as such involved." [3] About one fifth of the population is employed in the fisheries and the processing industries connected with fishing. By the 1950s, for the first time in the island's history, a substantial part of Iceland's population was urban.

Iceland's economic growth has been retarded, however, by a number of circumstances. The population and domestic market are small and roads and other means of transportation are not yet adequately developed (partly because of the size and partly because of the mountainous character of the country) to bring the population centers closer together. Water-power resources, though extensive, still remain largely unused. The climate is at times inclement enough to impose difficulties and suffering upon the inhabitants. Yet the Icelanders have reached a per capita income and general standard of living as high as those in the larger Western countries.

Iceland experienced a notable economic boom during the war years. Employment was high, the price level of export products rose steadily, the fish catches were good, and foreign fishing competition

[2] Dr. B. Eiriksson, in Skandinaviska Banken's *Quarterly Review*, XXXVI, 3 (July 1955), 76.
[3] *Iceland, Economic Program 1963-1966.* Statement by the Government to the Althing, April 10, 1963 (Reykjavik, 1963), p. 20.

on Icelandic fishing waters had been sharply reduced. The presence of tens of thousands of Allied troops created unprecedented demands for roads, airfields, barracks, and other types of construction that led to wages unheard of before the war. The island's good fortune, however, turned out to be a mixed blessing: a costly inflation was part of the price paid for the new prosperity. By the spring of 1946, the price level was nearly three times as high as it had been in the 1930s; by 1948, it was well over three times as high. Inflation has remained a heritage of the war and a pressing problem during the last two decades.

Other factors have further complicated the post-1945 situation. The nation's economy has remained unstable. The main reason is that the Icelanders are dependent upon a few export commodities. With only some 20 per cent of the population directly dependent on fishing and fish-processing, this branch of the island's economy provides well over 90 per cent of all exports. Another dimension of the situation is revealed by the fact that Iceland exports about 40 per cent of her gross national product. The failure of a summer herring season (and there have been several since 1945) and international crises such as the Korean War which caused a marked rise in the price of Iceland's imports, have produced great difficulties. These difficulties have been compounded by the fact that, as regards foods, the small nation is self-sufficient in milk and meat—and in fish, of course—but imports all cereals and fruits and some vegetables. Raw materials, oils, lubricants, machinery, feeds, and fertilizers are indispensable items in the list of imports. Although the over-all situation improved after 1954, the upward swing recorded by the mid-1960s was, on the whole, relatively slow.

Meantime, the economically backward Iceland of the turn of the century has largely disappeared, even in a physical sense. Most of the traditional sod houses are gone; concrete house and barn dominate much of the scene because there are no forests and therefore no wood building materials. A modern fishing fleet, an expanding merchant marine, an airlines network successfully contending for international patronage and trade, modern deep-freezing plants and other facilities necessary for the "fish economy" of the island—all testify to the long distance that separates the Iceland of the 1960's from the Iceland of 1900. They also strikingly illustrate the dependence of modern nations upon mutually advantageous international commercial exchange.

# NINE

# FOREIGN POLICY TRENDS SINCE 1945

*Problems and Prospects Before 1949*

When the war ended in 1945, the nations of the North faced a broad range of international problems. The approaches used and the policies formulated were largely determined by the differing experiences of each of the four states during the war. Denmark and Norway had been members of the grand alliance against Germany. Both had suffered five long years of harsh German occupation. Recognized as full-fledged Allied powers, they looked forward to the post-1945 advantages that membership in the coalition of victors would offer. Restitution and reparation for damage and losses suffered at the hands of the Germans could be expected, it was assumed, during the years that lay ahead. Security arrangements—in the making of which they themselves would have a hand—would be, they had every reason to expect, a part of the new order worked out by the Western powers.

Finland's position was quite different. Although the nation had escaped Soviet occupation, the war had imposed crushing burdens upon a people who had strained all resources to the utmost in fighting the Soviets. The reparations exactions, ominous even in the broad phrasing of the September 1944 armistice terms, appeared nothing less than crushing when set forth in detail in the reparations schedules presented by the Soviet Union in December of the same year. The other terms of the armistice agreement called for territorial cessions that meant the loss of about 12 per cent of the nation's territory (and the displacement of over 400,000 persons who chose to leave their homes rather than become Soviet citizens) and seemed to expose the country to further dangers from the East. Although the Allies knew full well that Soviet aggression and not Finnish intiative had drawn Finland into the war, the Finns had no opportunity to benefit from this knowledge. The fact that Finland had fought on the same side as Germany against the Soviet Union—although not against Western forces—unavoidably worked to the country's disadvantage after 1945. The Soviet Union could enforce its exactions upon the victim of its own aggression, unhindered by the Western powers without whose economic resources (American lend-lease alone to the Soviets amounted to $11 billion) and military might, expended in the effort to defeat Hitler, Germany would possibly have emerged victorious in Eastern Europe and the Soviet Union.

Sweden, favored by circumstances, had remained outside the war-time community of nations. Despite the great difficulties caused by Germany's military victories and seeming ascendancy is Europe in 1939-44, Sweden had manfully adhered to her policy of neutrality, although the policy at no time disguised her acceptance of the cause of the democratic West. When the war ended, Sweden was the only Scandinavian nation whose territorial and political pre-1939 status remained intact, while her neighbors faced the immense problems of reconstruction and rehabilitation imposed on them by foreign aggression.

Before 1939, the foreign policy of the Scandinavian states had largely ignored two important questions: common defense, and common economic policies. Although the latter had been periodically discussed, nothing concrete had been achieved when the war began. The Cold War has given new content and meaning to both questions. It also divided Scandinavia on the defense issue: Denmark and Norway joined the Western military alliance, Sweden and Finland did not.

The basic purposes of Scandinavian postwar foreign policy have been the same as those of the policy during the interwar years: to defend national security and independence, to avoid conflicts, and to remain on friendly terms with other states. These purposes are not matters of abstract choice; they are dictated by concrete national interests. The policy of peaceful relations with all nations implies the scrupulous observance of international commitments and obligations, strict neutrality and noninvolvement if foreign powers became embroiled in war. It also implies the acceptance of peaceful settlement of international disputes in which they themselves might become involved. This was impressively demonstrated in the Åland Island dispute between Sweden and Finland in 1921, in the conflicting Danish and Norwegian claims over Greenland, settled in 1933,[1] and in the

---

[1] During World War II, the United States obtained bases in Greenland. Greenland was placed within the Western Hemisphere security area in the Rio de Janeiro Pact of 1947, and American bases have been maintained in Greenland since Denmark joined NATO.

arrangements (1920-25) that recognized Svalbard as being under Norway's administration and sovereignty.

When the United Nations was formed in San Francisco in 1945, Denmark and Norway participated in the conference as members of the wartime alliance. Sweden, one of the first noncharter states to become a member, joined in October 1946. Finland's membership was delayed until 1955 by Big-Power frictions and disagreements that led the Soviet Union to veto for several years the admission of Finland and a number of other states.

Important as the United Nations has been since 1945 in encouraging international collaboration and peace, the Scandinavians concluded shortly after the war that it is unable, by itself, to guarantee peace and the security of small nations. This conclusion precipitated a new examination of Northern security and related requirements. It led, among other things, to the question of a pact providing for a common Scandinavian defensive alliance.

The problem of a common Scandinavian defense arrangement had been considered several years earlier. At the time when the first phase of the Russo-Finnish war was ending (March 1940), the Finns, the Swedes, and the Norwegians gave thought to the possibility of a Northern defense alliance. The idea was abandoned, mainly because the Soviet Union chose to see in the contemplated arrangement a potential anti-Soviet alliance. The German invasion of Denmark and Norway shortly thereafter eliminated both these nations from potential participation in any Scandinavian defense scheme. In the autumn of 1940, Sweden and Finland considered a mutual defense arrangement involving not only a military pact but some form of political union as well. The Soviet Union considered this, too, a potential anti-Soviet conspiracy that would violate, as far as Finland was concerned, the peace treaty of March 12, 1940. Nothing therefore came of the idea, and it was not until 1948-49 that the question was raised once more. The main reason for its reappearance was the territorial expansion and general aggressive designs of international Communism.

### Norway, Denmark, and NATO

For a century and a quarter before 1940, Norway had not been involved in war. Neutrality in all international conflicts had become something of a national doctrine—or, as a commentator has aptly put it: "an unwritten part of the constitution." The German invasion and occupation shattered that doctrine and brought Norway into the ranks of the warring nations. A founder-member of the United Nations, Norway unhesitatingly accepted the obligations stated in the Charter, among them "to make available to the Security Council . . . armed forces, assistance, and facilities" necessary for dealing with acts of aggression and the maintenance of peace and security (Article 43). Denmark's position in 1945 was essentially the same as Norway's, and membership in the United Nations carried the same implications in both countries.

Participation in the United Nations in 1945 was not understood to involve, however, a complete abandonment of neutrality: the United Nations was an international organization, not an alliance. Because it was an international organization, membership in it was appropriate to noncommitted nations desirous of remaining outside Big-Power conflicts. When the Cold War changed the situation and created the East-West blocs, the question of national security requirements came to the fore in a new and insistent way. Norway and Denmark concluded that the United Nations could not be counted upon to provide essential security guarantees. The Communist coup in Czechoslovakia in February 1948 did much to decide the matter for both countries. The safest choice seemed to be an alliance with Western powers that could be assumed to be strong enough to prevent war and—in the event that war came—strong enough to offer protection to small as well as big powers. Norway and Denmark therefore joined NATO. In doing so, they embarked upon a new foreign policy that differed sharply from their peacetime foreign policy before 1939.

Unqualified as Denmark's and Norway's acceptance of the obligations of NATO membership has been, it has not prevented their continuing attention to changes in the general international situation. It is a fact worthy of note that, before the Hungarian revolt in October-November, 1956 and its suppression by Soviet forces, a good deal of discussion in both countries centered on the broad question of whether the possibilities of coexistence and national security might not call for a reconsideration of the long-range implications of membership in the Western military alliance. The events in Hungary ended the discussion but, in all likelihood, only postponed further consideration of these questions. The mere passage of time is likely to strengthen, rather than weaken, the neutralist inclinations of Denmark and Norway.

Iceland also became a member of NATO in 1949. When Iceland joined, it was agreed that foreign forces would be stationed in the island only with the country's permission and only in time of war.

(The same was true of Norway and Denmark.) In 1951, however, the United States and Iceland signed an agreement that allowed the stationing of American troops in Iceland. The agreement provided that it could be terminated eighteen months after Iceland had served notice of intention to cancel it.

In March 1956, the Icelandic legislature adopted a resolution calling for the withdrawal of the United States forces. The Council of NATO, requested by Iceland to review the necessity of continuing the defense facilities on the island, stated in July that they were still needed. It recommended that the 1951 arrangement "be continued in such a form . . . as will maintain the strength of the common defense."

The Council based its recommendation on its opinion that the world situation was still precarious and allowed no relaxation of the NATO members' vigilance. Before Iceland took further action in the matter, and as if to buttress the Council's view, the Hungarian revolt offered ample proof that the situation in Eastern Europe was far from tranquil and that Soviet aggressive designs were by no means a thing of the past. Iceland therefore abandoned the effort to oust the American troops, and the 1951 agreement remained in force.

The Icelanders' aversion to foreign troops is understandable. They have long felt that the continued presence of foreign troops threatens important aspects of their national life. For instance, much of Iceland's economy has become dependent on the American military base. This has posed a serious problem, for American expenditures since 1951 have continued and increased the ominous inflation that followed in the wake of the last war. Other, noneconomic, considerations are also involved. The nation is small, the foreign troops relatively large in numbers. Iceland, it is held by many patriotic Icelanders, can retain its proud and ancient culture, and can maintain its sharply defined linguistic separateness—that is, the very foundations of its national existence—only by jealously guarding itself against the corrosive effects of foreign influence. Thus national and nationalistic considerations in Iceland also sustain a latent, markedly neutralist inclination. It is likely to grow rather than decline unless the international situation continues to accent Iceland's and NATO's military defense establishment needs in a manner that reduces other concerns to secondary importance.

### Sweden's Neutrality Policy

In Sweden, neutrality is not only an inclination, but an established policy commitment, carefully and rationally planned and resolutely carried through. Sweden also faced, in 1948, the question of neutrality versus alliance or close political cooperation with the Western powers. Several events brought the question to the fore after the war ended in 1945. Outstanding among them were the mounting evidence of Communist aggression, illustrated especially by the coup in Czechoslovakia in February 1948, and the discussions and moves that led, in April 1949, to the formation of NATO. Sweden's official reaction to these developments at once underlined her resolve to remain neutral. This was made clear in a statement of Foreign Minister Ö. Unden in February 1948: "The Government is convinced that the overwhelming majority of the Swedish people do not wish to join any great power bloc, either by a specific treaty or alliance or by silent acquiescence in joint military measures in the event of a conflict." He went on to say that if the United Nations acts "according to its program" in international conflicts, Sweden would observe "the obligations which United Nations membership imposes." If, however, the United Nations "is being undermined by the creation of political blocs," Sweden must be free "to choose the road of neutrality. . . . We do not wish, through commitments in advance, to renounce the right and the chance to stay outside another war."

The choice of neutrality as the sheet anchor of national security was not inflexible, however. Later in the year Sweden joined Norway and Denmark in discussions regarding the possibilities of Scandinavian military cooperation. In January 1949, as a result of the discussions, Sweden offered her two neighbors a ten-year military alliance. The suggestion marked a sharp deviation from Sweden's traditional neutrality policy of the past century and a half. The main purpose of the Swedish proposal, to keep Scandinavia free of Big-Power entanglements, was accented by that part of the proposal which obligated the members of the intended alliance not to accept any military commitments that would bind them to other countries. In Sweden's view, the alliance would serve to keep the three member nations out of war unless attacked. It was also assumed that the alliance might receive military materiel from the United States.

Nothing came of the Swedish proposal; Norway concluded, as has been suggested, that a purely Scandinavian alliance was not sufficient to safeguard national security. In January 1949, the United States made it clear that American military supplies would be made available only to countries associated with its collective security arrangements. This announcement led Norway and Denmark to reconsider the terms on which the two countries might join in the

NATO discussions, and both finally signed the pact on April 4, 1949. The decision to join was supported by the two national legislatures; only the Communist members (apparently acting according to the preferences of Moscow) voted against the proposal. Sweden, on the other hand, decided to stay out of the alliance—a decision supported by a seemingly overwhelming majority of the nation.

The motives behind Sweden's neutrality in international affairs are clear enough and, for nearly two decades, have been unanimously recognized as valid by all political parties in the country.

The tradition of neutrality is often mentioned as a reason for the decision to take a neutral position in the post-1948 world. Yet it is clear that Sweden's choice is not based on an uncritical faith in miracles or a naïve belief that past good fortune will automatically continue and keep the country out of future wars. The country's position rests on sober analyses and careful conclusions directly related to the realities of the Big-Power line-up during the last war and the realities of the Cold War of the past two decades.

Outstanding among these conclusions is the belief that to link Sweden's—or, for that matter, Scandinavia's—defense requirements with those of the Atlantic alliance is to increase the danger of war, not to avoid it. The chance to stay out of war should not be given up before the threat of involvement actually develops. Membership in NATO would mean the surrender, in advance, of all opportunity to avoid war, and the automatic extension of the Cold War to Sweden. Nor would Sweden's membership in the Western alliance increase the chances of securing peace; on the contrary, it would make the country's involvement in war inevitable. The alliance, dominated by the Big Powers, could not be expected to give Sweden a decisive voice in situations that might determine her own involvement in war. Sweden would have to accept the results of Big-Power conflicts over matters of no direct concern to her without materially increasing her own ability to ward off or survive attack. Developments in nuclear rocketry merely reinforce this conclusion. One of the consequences of membership in NATO would be the establishment of missile bases within Sweden. Missile bases are areas that will unquestionably be primary targets in a new war. Thus Sweden in NATO would be in the category of countries first to draw fire. Sweden conspicuously and unqualifiedly neutral and firmly resolved to use her considerable defense potential in meeting violations of her neutrality, however, is seen as occupying the safest international position available to a small power recognized by all states as a foe of every form of aggression and a supporter of every effort designed to enlarge the area of peace and concord in the world.

These views and conclusions imply no ideological neutrality or wavering in the East-West conflict. No secret has been made today of Sweden's unqualified acceptance of the values and principles on which Western democratic societies rest. Neutralism is, in the Swedish view, entirely compatible with devotion to the principles of the free world. And neutralism, buttressed by a firm resolve to maintain strong national defenses, might well turn out to contribute more to international stability and peace than a policy that perpetuates the hardening of international alignments. Continued adherence to alliance-free neutrality is therefore seen as morally acceptable and as rationally defensible. The Swedes—and the Finns also—stand no less erect among the free nations than those whose choices during the last war contributed not a little to the emergence of the dangers NATO is expected to minimize and, ultimately, to overcome.

### Finland's Position

Finland's international position and policies since 1945, like those of the other Scandinavian nations, have reflected the consequences of the Cold War. Especially during the years before the onerous reparations bill had been paid in full, the Finns displayed a firm resolve to do nothing that might disturb relations with the Soviet Union. For example, in the summer of 1947, Finland was invited, along with twenty other nations, to discuss questions relating to joining the Marshall Plan. The government and the legislature favored participation, but the final decision was negative. The reason was, as the official statement put it, that the plan, "having become a source of serious differences of opinion among the Big Powers [i.e., the Soviet Union having objected to the plan], Finland, desiring to remain outside the areas of conflict in Big-Power politics" regretfully would not take part in the discussions. The Finns therefore did not benefit from the economic assistance provided by the Marshall Plan to the Western nations of postwar Europe.

A similar hands-off attitude was shown by the Finns in 1948-49, when the Northern democracies contemplated the formation of a defensive neutrality bloc free from Big-Power affiliations. The Soviet Union insisted that the plan meant only a military coalition serving Western "imperialist" anti-Soviet purposes. The cautious Finns thereupon decided not to take part in the negotiations (which, as has been noted, ultimately failed for other reasons).

A new element in Finnish-Soviet relations emerged early in 1948, when Stalin proposed that Finland and the Soviet Union conclude "a mutual assistance pact . . . against possible German attack." The proposal caused extensive discussion and not a little unease in Finland. Except for the Communists, ever ready to follow Moscow's lead, public opinion was opposed to the pact. There being no convenient alternative, the government decided to avoid arousing Soviet suspicions and enmity and accepted Stalin's suggestion. A ten-year agreement of "friendship, cooperation, and mutual assistance" was signed on April 6, 1948, after negotiations that turned out to be more successful in securing Finland's neutral position than most observers could have confidently assumed at the time.

The treaty stated that, if Finland "or the Soviet Union through Finland" is attacked by Germany or any state allied with Germany, "Finland will fight" to resist the attack "within the borders of Finland" and, if necessary, "with the assistance of the Soviet Union." The question of if and when Soviet aid might be given will be decided by "mutual agreement." If a threat of military attack appeared, the two signatories would "consult each other." Both agreed "loyally to participate," in accordance with "the aims and principles" of the United Nations, in all available measures for keeping the peace. Alliances directed against the other signatory were forbidden, and the obligation to respect "the sovereignty and integrity" and "noninterference in the internal affairs" of the other party to the treaty was also mutually accepted.

The 1948 pact has been frequently mentioned as the cornerstone of Finland's postwar foreign policy, and it has at times been interpreted as an agreement that makes possible Soviet infringement upon the republic's freedom of action in foreign relations. Developments since 1948 have clarified the matter in many respects. It seems obvious that the treaty has not changed Finland's basic position: treaty or no treaty, the Finns would fight to the best of their ability against any invader. In its provision of possible Soviet aid after "mutual agreement," the treaty adds nothing of substance to the realities of the post-1945 world. Either "mutual agreement" will mean cooperation in opposing an invader in the sense stated in the treaty or, if these words turn out to be meaningless, Finland will have been reduced, by the time an invasion comes, to a Soviet-imposed servitude (not caused by the treaty but by Soviet action prior to the moment of invasion) that deprives the Finns of a free choice and leaves the decisions wholly in the hands of the Soviet Union. Finally, a German attack upon Finland or an invasion of the Soviet Union through Finland appear to be so remote as to invite the conclusion that the "invasion clauses" of the treaty lack real meaning.

Since 1948, Finland has seen in the treaty a commitment limited to the defense of her own territory—one in no way incompatible with a policy of neutrality. On the contrary, the pact is considered a guarantee of neutrality and is clearly different from the treaties of mutual assistance the Soviet Union has concluded with several of the satellite nations. The treaty is held to be especially important in creating and maintaining Soviet confidence in Finland's firm resolve to remain outside Big-Power conflicts and to follow a policy of nonalignment that contributes to and secures peaceful coexistence between the republic and the Soviet Union. It also leaves Finland free to remain neutral in all instances of actual or potential Soviet military conflicts that do not involve Finland's own territory.

In 1955, a year that marked a substantial improvement in Finland's postwar status, the treaty was extended for twenty years. The Porkkala enclave, only some dozen miles west of Helsinki, had been leased to the Soviet Union for a naval base in 1944. It represented a galling and dangerous territorial servitude. The Soviets agreed to return the area to Finland in 1955, and did so the following year. The abandonment of Porkkala by the Soviets was widely seen as an indication of lessened Soviet suspicions of Finland, a measure of the improvement in the relations of the two countries, and as an illustration of peaceful coexistence undisturbed by Soviet hostility.

For thirteen years, the treaty introduced no new problems in Finnish-Soviet relations. Finland's sovereignty remained as inviolate as it had been before the spring of 1948. The completion of the reparations payments in 1952 and the return of Porkkala four years later went a long way toward easing Finland's position.

On October 30, 1961, however, a Soviet note appeared to inject a new aspect into the relations between the two states. The October 1961 note invoked the 1948 treaty for the first time (and to date the only time). Inspired by Cold War problems in Berlin, over nine tenths of the note was a lengthy indictment of Western "warmongers and imperialists." NATO members Denmark and Norway were accused of assisting in the revival of a militarist Germany again emerging as a threat to the peace of Europe. Swedish munitions manufacturers and other "interests" were, it was claimed, also involved. Because of these and related developments, the Soviet Union asserted, a situation was emerging that threatened the security of both countries and required consultations on the basis of the 1948 pact.

The note led to a suggestion by President U. Kekkonen that the questions raised by it be discussed between Premier N. Khrushchev and himself. The suggestion was accepted. The discussions resulted in an understanding announced in an official communiqué of November 25, 1961. It stated that the Soviets had confidence in Finland's strict neutrality policy and could therefore "put off the military conversations it had proposed." Thus the immediate results of the note did not change, but underlined, Finland's commitment to unqualified neutrality. Its long-range implications cannot yet be discerned, but it appears abundantly clear that they will not change the nation's conviction and resolve that neutrality in general and friendly relations with the Soviet Union in particular are the alpha and the omega of Finland's foreign policy.

The fact that Denmark, Norway, and Iceland are in NATO while Sweden and Finland cling to neutrality defined by postwar developments offers a measure of the differences in views among these nations regarding the requirements of national interest and security. Yet a marked unanimity of basic purpose in fact prevails. The essence of the matter was stated, some years ago, by a Danish observer who remarked:

> It is only in approach and not in objectives that the Nordic countries hold differing views in foreign policy. Their fundamental attitude . . . is identical. They have one overriding interest and one goal: to preserve peace. This is a traditional policy of the Nordic countries. . . . In the present constellation of powers each Nordic country has taken the position it finds best for its own safety, for the cause of peace, and for the interests of the other Nordic peoples. And the resolve to work for peace and democratic ideals is identical in all five states.[2]

The Scandinavians' United Nations policy has illustrated the unambiguous determination to avoid decisions and actions likely to increase international friction and discord. Although Denmark and Norway—as members of NATO—have been concerned with matters involving military policy and commitments, the general policy of the four states has been to remain outside the controversies of the Big

[2] F. Wendt, in *The Nordic Council and Cooperation in Scandinavia* (Copenhagen: Munksgaard, 1959), p. 235.

Powers. In general, they have preferred to support realistic plans for peace while shying away from high-flown proclamations and purposes that offer little or no possibility of concrete achievement. Finland, in particular, has abstained from "moral indictments" of governments or condemnation of the internal policies of member states, holding that the United Nations has no authority, as Article 7 of the Charter puts it, "to intervene in matters which are essentially within the domestic jurisdiction of any state." Within the United Nations organization, the Scandinavian states have given continuing evidence of cooperation. Frequent—at times daily—consultation among the members of the four delegations appear to have become routine ways of attending to their United Nations business. In this respect they follow the pattern suggested by the periodic meetings and conferences of Scandinavian premiers and foreign ministers that have become a regular feature of Northern cooperation in foreign relations.

### Scandinavia "Between East and West"?

The question of Scandinavia as "between East and West" could hardly have been raised before World War II, and had it been raised, it would in all likelihood have been dismissed as devoid of substance and meaning. Before the war, the four nations of the North were—in all respects that have meaning for the East-versus-West concept—wholly a part of the West. Conceptions of freedom and liberty, government and political institutions, religion and the church, education and the role of school and university, the press and other organs of public opinion, the place of law and the courts in a society of free men—all conformed to "Western" patterns evolved long before 1918. Their further development during the interwar years rested on no formulae or prescriptions derived from the Communist world or Eastern Europe.

The European power constellation since 1945 has given rise to the classification of nations as "Western," "Eastern," or "between East and West." Considerations of national security—not ideological affinities or preferences—have led to the choices made and affiliations sought by Denmark, Norway, and Sweden. And although post-1945 circumstances influencing Finland's foreign-policy orientation have obviously been partly different from those seen as decisive by her Western neighbors, the safety and security needs of the republic and not political or social philosophy as such have dictated the course followed by Helsinki. Finland is not a border area between East and West in which, as some commentators have claimed, the problems of coexistence are an old and basically unchanging aspect of the nation's life.[3] Such a view or interpretation is likely to obscure the fact that Finland has been a part of the West throughout her recorded history and that, in Finland's case, *coexistence* has meaning only if the word is used as a synonym for a situation created by Soviet aggression.

It is thus clear that Denmark and Norway in NATO and Sweden and Finland outside the Western military coalition, determined to follow the path marked out by their neutrality policies, has not meant that the four countries have assumed basically different positions in the East-West conflict of political ideas. Their positions in this area have not been middle positions that enable them to provide mediating services in a divided Europe. And it is clear that only the Communists in Scandinavia, who are a minority even in Finland, have abandoned the solid anchorage of Western democratic ideas and practices. As regards the driving and creative forces in the field of economic activity, it is individual initiative and enterprise—not centrally controlled state socialism—that dominates the scene. The high degree of postwar political stability in the North (especially marked in view of the unease and upheavals in many other parts of Europe), the general economic prosperity testifying to continuing improvement in the standard of living, and the vigorous cultural advances of the past two decades can be more readily understood if these basic features of Scandinavian foreign policy are kept in mind.

[3] See, for instance, Anatole Mazour's *Finland Between East and West* (New York: D. Van Nostrand Co., Inc., 1950).

# TEN

# SCANDINAVIAN UNITY AND COOPERATION

## Bases for Unity

Many observers of the Scandinavian nations, especially since World War II, have been impressed by the many evidences of Scandinavian unity. More frequently than not, the wide area of co-operation among the nations of the North has been explained as a consequence of their linguistic unity. The explanation is inadequate at best and fails to account for other, more decisive factors—which, for want of a better word, may be called *historical*.

At one time, the people of Scandinavia (except the Finns) had little difficulty in understanding each other. By the fifteenth century, how-ever, substantial differentiation had developed, and distinctive Danish, Norwegian, and Swedish languages had emerged at the time of the Reformation. The translation of the Bible into the vernacular—during the second quarter of the sixteenth century, and the publication there-after of religious literature, sharpened the distinctions. Especially since the first half of the nineteenth century, the differences have become still more sharply etched and, in some respects, continue to grow rather than diminish.

Norway and Finland in particular illustrate the complexities of the language problem among the Scandinavian family of nations. The union of Norway and Denmark lasted from the end of the fourteenth century until 1814. During the greater part of the centuries before 1814, Norway was little more than a province ruled from or by Copen-hagen. One of the results of this state of affairs was that Danish be-came the language of government, education, and so-called polite society in general while the Norwegian literary language—closely akin to Icelandic—fell into disuse. The fact that Norway had no university of her own before 1811 also increased her cultural de-pendence on Denmark. The new literature that was stimulated by the Reformation and that reached and influenced Norway was written in

Danish; most of the members of the clergy were either Danes or Danish-educated Norwegians. Government, laws, decrees, administration, and the like meant the use of Danish, not Norwegian. Norwegian dialects remained the language of the common folk while the upper classes spoke Danish—although it was a Danish markedly influenced by Norwegian.

The end of the union with Denmark in 1814 and the beginning of the ninety years of union with Sweden marked the opening of a new stage in the development of the Norwegian language. The separation from Denmark and the new affiliation with Sweden—which most Norwegians would have been glad to avoid—made it inevitable that the Norwegians would sooner or later begin to appraise their "Danish" past and to anticipate the consequences of the union with Sweden in a manner that would create a new and quickened national consciousness. To free the nation from Danish linguistic and cultural influences, and at the same time to avoid "corruption" by and amalgamation with the Swedes, became a major concern of the many Norwegians who emerged, after 1814, as the spokesmen of the new nationalist dispensation.

One of the consequences of the attempts at language reform fostered by Norwegian patriots after 1814 was the emergence, by about the middle of the nineteenth century, of a "language conflict" destined to leave a deep impression upon many aspects of Norwegian literary and cultural life. Some advocated the creation and use of a written Norwegian language wholly based upon the indigenous Norwegian spoken by the peasants. This language came to be known as *Landsmaal* or *Neo-Norwegian*. Others again urged that written Dano-Norwegian be taken as the basis, with its orthography changed to correspond to Norwegian pronunciation and the adoption of new words and forms from native Norwegian dialects. The conflict intensified after 1885 and a number of parliamentary committees were set up to investigate and propose spelling reforms, and several official reforms in spelling were introduced (in 1907, 1917, 1938). In 1951, the government appointed a permanent Linguistic Commission, to provide more fixed and satisfactory standards for the two "languages," both of which have been officially recognized in the schools for several years. Rules for uniform standards were published by the Commission in 1958 and authorized by the Ministry of Education in the same year. These accomplishments have by no means solved the problem or ended the "language conflict."

Norway, sovereign since 1905, fully free to originate and sustain a far-reaching language reform—and, incidentally, a significant cultural renaissance accenting truly national features—has been an active participant in the development of Scandinavian unity during the past two generations in a manner that would probably have been impossible before she had freed herself from what were seen as linguistic and related encumbrances of Danish origin. In this participation, language relationships have been secondary to considerations anchored in other concerns of state and nation.

Finland offers another illustration of the role of history as contrasted with language relationships in the development of Northern unity. If language were the sole or main requisite of unity, Finland would be largely outside the Scandinavian family of nations. Yet the fact is that Finland is a charter member of the Nordic group. The membership is decreed by the verdict of history.

It bears repeating that, before 1809, Finland was an integral part of the Swedish realm. Finland was not "controlled by" or "under" Sweden; it was not a subordinate province ruled from Stockholm. The inhabitants of the Finnish part of the kingdom were, in law and in fact, Swedes as regards the rights of the individual, the privileges of cities or of the four-Estate Riksdag. Representation in the Riksdag was never denied to the Finns any more than to the Swedes; appointments to public office, whether in the service of state or church, followed no official "nationality" line. Many of the outstanding figures in Swedish history were Finns who served king and country with distinction and made contributions in the field of science, letters, and the arts; conversely, not a few leading men in Finnish history had been born and reared west of the Gulf of Bothnia. During the generations when Finland and Sweden formed a single state, Sweden and Finland evolved a common system of law, courts, administration, and government at the local and national level, as well as religious and educational institutions upon which both nations built after 1809. It is, then, because of the basic and continuing features of Finland's political, educational, and religious institutions and way of life—and the preferences and inclinations created and solidified by them— that Finland today displays an indelible Northern stamp.

It bears emphasizing also that this Northern stamp does not depend merely on the fact that the native language of over 300,000 citizens of Finland is Swedish. Some commentators on Finland state or imply that it is this part of Finland's population that connects Finland with her neighbors to the west and that, without them, Finland would be outside the Nordic fold. The assumption is unwarranted, for two reasons. First, the Swede-Finns as a group have never been the spokesmen or representatives of Finland as a whole. During the union with Sweden, they never enjoyed any special privileges or status denied the rest of the Finns. Neither in law nor in government, administration, or life in general were they considered or treated as a "nationality" separate from their Finnish-speaking compatriots. The same is true today: both language groups are equally citizens in a free republic and the linguistic rights of the minority are guaranteed by the republican constitution of 1919.

Second, the educated class in Finland is, for all practical purposes, bilingual, speaking both Swedish and Finnish. The constitution, in conferring official status on Swedish as well as on Finnish obviously refers, in constitutional idiom, to a language situation of decisive importance. One of its consequences is that graduates of secondary schools and universities, no matter whether their "home language" is Finnish or Swedish, know both languages. Complete bilingualism is common, and is often found even among individuals with only moderate schooling. It is from the ranks of the bilingual groups that Finland has drawn the main talent and leadership needed for continuing and successful participation in the common concerns and purposes of the Scandinavian family of peoples. This is one way of saying that the fact that over nine tenths of Finland's population is Finnish in speech has not prevented Finland's membership in the Scandinavian group, and that, on the other hand, the Swede-Finn element as such is not the custodian of Finland's Scandinavian interests. These interests are in the keeping of a part of the nation—educated and leading elements in general—that is in no sense coterminous with the Swede-Finn group as a whole.

At one time, the Danes and the Swedes regarded one another as hereditary enemies. In his perceptive Foreword to Franklin D. Scott's excellent *The United States and Scandinavia*, the former President of the American-Scandinavian Foundation, Lithgow Osborne—himself an outstanding student of Scandinavia—summarized this long and tragic chapter in the history of the North: "These countries . . . participated in dreary generations of feuds and wars, dynastic and religious. Sometimes allied, more frequently fighting one another; sometimes teamed up with one great power against another, and later shifting sides." [1] The long period from the fifteenth to the early

[1] Franklin D. Scott, *The United States and Scandinavia* (Cambridge, Mass.: Harvard University Press, 1950), p. xiv. Sweden and Finland, to be sure, never fought one another, and the same is true of Norway and Denmark since the Middle Ages.

nineteenth century was periodically punctuated by wars and coalitions in which the two peoples were repeatedly at one another's throats. Norwegians were often involved and had to bear part of the burdens and costs of Swedish-Danish rivalries. The main territorial losses suffered by Denmark in modern times were caused by Swedish seventeenth-century conquests and policies which, incidentally, gave Sweden her present western and southern boundaries and separated Norway from Denmark. It was not until after 1814 that the divisive influences of these earlier historical experiences began to vanish, especially during the middle decades of the past century when "Scandinavianism" —in the modern sense of the word—first made its appearance. Much of this Scandinavian movement was centered in the universities and was sustained by university students and graduates. It subsided after the mid-1860s and left no important legacy of practical or workable Scandinavian cooperation. The dissolution of the Swedish-Norwegian union in 1905 seemed to place additional obstacles in the way of the slowly expanding unofficial forms of cooperation that emerged after the 1870s. The problems and difficulties of World War I, however, led Norway, Sweden, and Denmark to cooperate in the attempt to overcome the hardships which the war imposed on the Nordic neutrals. Although "a common language" and alleged "common origin" had failed to induce close cooperation in questions of vital national concern, the harsh realities of the war led to intergovernmental and other forms of collaboration, especially in the common defense of neutrality.

Scandinavian cooperation was substantially broadened during the interwar years, reflecting in many ways the Scandinavians' deepening sense of solidarity. One of its main sources of strength was the Norden Society, an organization with branches in the four countries and Iceland. Its national organizations number over 500 and its membership, composed largely of influential cultural, political, and business leaders, and other public figures, exceeds 120,000. Conferences, lectures, and cultural exchanges covering a wide variety of activities loom large on its program. Significant among its many enterprises is the revision of history textbooks in order to correct and eliminate narrow nationalist interpretations of the past and to broaden the areas of tolerance and appreciative understanding of the neighbors' history and achievements.

The Northern Interparliamentary Union, a number of nonofficial industrial and trade associations, and close cooperation among Scandinavian labor unions and professional organizations testified to other aspects of the broadening front covering wide areas of interest.

In 1934, the five governments (Iceland was also included) authorized the setting up of special Delegations for the Promotion of Economic Cooperation. Many economic problems of common interest were considered at the Conference of the Delegations and resulted, among other things, in a publication that dealt with these problems and was itself an illustration of the growing cooperation among these five nations.[2]

### The Nordic Council

A significant aspect of Scandinavian developments since 1945 is the broadening field of Nordic cooperation. Neither the divergent war-time experiences of the Scandinavian nations nor the different domestic and foreign affairs problems that have held the stage since 1945 have narrowed or destroyed collaboration among them. On the contrary, the years since the late 1940s have testified to a strengthened solidarity and resolve to join hands not only in pursuing purely Scandinavian purposes but in dealing with questions of wider international import as well.

The most striking post-1945 achievement in the field of Scandinavian cooperation is the Nordic Council. It owes its existence largely to the efforts of the late Prime Minister Hans Hedtoft of Denmark. An enthusiastic spokesman for close Scandinavian cooperation, he was the guiding spirit in the unsuccessful effort in the late 1940s to create a common defense policy for the North. At a meeting of the Northern Interparliamentary Union in 1951, he proposed meetings of members of the national parliaments, to be held regularly, at which purposes common to the North could be discussed and pursued. The parliaments of Denmark, Norway, Iceland, and Sweden accepted the idea, and the first session of the Nordic Council was held in Copenhagen in February 1953. Finland joined in 1955.

The Statute of the Nordic Council defines it as a consultative body set up by the legislatures of the five countries. Its membership consists of sixteen members from each of the parliaments of Denmark, Finland, Norway, and Sweden, and five from that of Iceland. Cabinet ministers appointed by the five governments also attend— they usually number about thirty—and normally include the premier and the foreign minister of each country. Cabinet ministers freely participate in the discussions of the Council and may be invited to sit in on committee meetings, but they have no vote. Members of the Council are seated alphabetically, not by country. The delega-

[2] *The Northern Countries in World Economy* (Helsinki: Otava, 1937).

tions from each country are chosen by the national parliaments; the membership of each delegation reflects the party constellation within the legislature. The delegations have consistently included leading members of the individual parties. The Council meets once a year, for one week, alternating among the capitals of Denmark, Finland, Norway, and Sweden (the size and accommodations of Reykjavik in Iceland have prevented regular sessions there).

In principle, the Council is concerned "only with current problems, that is, with problems considered suitable for immediate and specific action." It should "abstain from making declarations" regarding purposes and objectives for which "no immediate measures can be proposed." The self-imposed limitations of the Council's agenda include military questions and the relations of the five nations with non-Scandinavian states. The reason for the limitation is that the Scandinavian countries have not followed a common defense or foreign-relations policy: Denmark and Norway are members of NATO; Sweden has sought refuge in "alliance-free neutrality"; and Finland has committed herself to strict neutrality, with a special accent on her relations with the Soviet Union.

Because the Nordic Council is a purely advisory body, its proposals and resolutions are not binding upon the member countries. Yet there is more to the Council than its statutes suggest. It can and does present recommendations to the governments. Its recommendations, emerging as they do from discussions in which all member states have equal representation and participation, enjoy great prestige. At the session following that in which the recommendation was made, the governments are obligated to report the action taken. Only the elected members and the representatives of the governments are competent to bring proposals before the Council. The items on the agenda may deal with all five countries, or with only two (or three or four) of them. After detailed discussion of a matter duly submitted in appropriate committees, the Council indulges in full-scale debate in a plenary session. The committees—each of which deals with legal, social, cultural, economic, or communications questions—are assisted in their labors by experts provided by the various governments.

Since it began to function in 1953, the Nordic Council has initiated or taken part in a wide variety of policies and measures that have substantially expanded the area of collaboration among its member states. By the end of 1961, the Council had authored 186 recommendations submitted to two or more of the five nations. The recommendations covered nearly 250 subjects. Of the total, fifty-nine had been fully accepted and forty-nine partly carried through by the governments involved. Meantime, the purposes of seventeen others had been reached without action by the governments. The recommendations dealt with questions that ranged from general education, various fields of science, law, taxation, radio and television, railroad traffic and rates, and the employment of nurses and midwives, to questions of foreign exchange, atomic energy, and Scandinavian water-power resources. During the first decade of its existence, about one third of the Council's recommendations dealing with economic or social policy matters, and well over half of those dealing with law or traffic and communications, were favorably acted upon.

Partly as a result of the endeavors of the Nordic Council, and partly as the consequence of efforts originating and carried forward outside the Council, a growing body of legislative and other measures has notably expanded the area of cooperation among the Northern states. In some significant respects, the national boundaries separating the four nations have been erased: passports were abolished in 1952; drivers' licenses of one Scandinavian country are accepted in all the others; customs inspection of non-Scandinavians is limited to the point of entry and is not repeated at the border of the other countries; a free, common labor market—except for certain professions—established in 1954, has meant the abolition of work permits and the opening of jobs to nationals of all the Northern nations. The boundaries that divide Scandinavia into separate sovereignties have become formalities in other ways also: a Convention signed in 1956 provided that sickness, accident, old-age, maternity, and other social security benefits be extended, by the country of residence, without reference to citizenship, to Scandinavian nationals; the costs of these benefits are borne by the country of residence and not by the beneficiary's native country.

This is clearly a unique and important illustration of what might be called a new, emerging concept of citizenship. A Dane, a Finn, a Norwegian, or a Swede is entitled, while a resident in a Scandinavian country other than his own, to benefits and advantages normally provided by public authority only for citizens. This suggests the beginnings of a common citizenship. The fact that it is limited to benefits provided by a certain category of social legislation, and involves no political rights, does not obscure the significance of this impressive illustration of the Scandinavians' capacity for mutually beneficial cooperation.

The resolve of the Nordic Council member nations to work together was demonstrated with exceptional emphasis at the 1962 annual session of the Council, that met in Helsinki on March 17th to 23rd. The session marked the tenth anniversary of the Council. It culminated in the signing of a special agreement, the Helsinki Convention, ratified in due time by the parliaments of the five nations. Its forty articles described the areas of existing cooperation and indicated guidelines for the future.

The signatories agreed to develop further cooperation in matters legal, cultural, social, and economic. They also agreed to work toward the establishment of the "greatest possible legal equality" between noncitizen Scandinavians residing in a Northern country and the citizens of that country; easier naturalization; mutual recognition and enforcement of "court verdicts, or decisions by some other authority"; the preservation and expansion of the common labor market and the mutual social benefits; and measures to encourage increased Scandinavian production and investment. Still another part of the Convention provided that a citizen of one Nordic country could, in certain circumstances, make use, while abroad, of the foreign-service facilities of a Northern country other than his own.[3]

## Economic Cooperation

In recent years, attempts to deal with economic questions of common interest have been numerous and markedly successful. The idea of Northern economic cooperation goes back decades and was particularly emphasized between the two wars. The war years 1939-45 interrupted developments in evidence before 1939, but these were revived not long after fighting had ceased. A special organ, the Joint Scandinavian Committee for Economic Cooperation—established in the spring of 1948 by Denmark, Norway, and Sweden—signalized a new interest in this vital question. The Joint Committee examined at length the bases for and the pros and cons of a Scandinavian customs union. The conclusions of the Committee pointed out that the economic interests of the North would be well served by the elimination of most, if not all, of the intra-Scandinavian tariffs, and by the introduction of uniform tariffs on imports from non-Scandinavian countries. The Joint Committee held, however, that, for the time being, a real Scandinavian customs union could not advantageously be established.

The question was later considered by the Nordic Council, especially

[3] This important Convention is given in the Appendix.

at its 1957 session in Helsinki. The result was a plan for a Common Scandinavian Market, to include Denmark, Finland, Norway, and Sweden. Before the plan had been fully worked out, however, questions relating to the establishment of a larger common market in western and central Europe emerged and overtook the Scandinavians' project. The larger common market was, in fact, established by the Rome Treaty signed on March 25, 1957, only about a month after the Nordic Council's Helsinki session. The so-called European Economic Community—the EEC—became a reality on January 1, 1958. These developments forced a reconsideration of the Scandinavian Common Market project, and it was abandoned. Ultimately, another so-called free-trade area, the European Free Trade Association—the EFTA—or "the Outer Seven," was set up. It was comprised of Britain, Denmark, Norway, Sweden, Switzerland, Portugal, and Austria. The treaty setting up the EFTA was signed on January 1, 1960, and went into effect a month later. Finland signed a special convention with the EFTA on March 27, 1961, and joined the group on July 1, 1961.

The most important feature of the EFTA agreement is the gradual abolition of tariff dues. According to the tariff time table accepted by the members of the Finn-EFTA, all levies will be abolished in their trade with each other by the end of 1969, when a genuine free-trade area comprising the eight nations will presumably have been fully established. Meantime, an increase in intra-Scandinavian trade has been recorded and appears to give promise of expanding considerably in years to come.

AN AGREEMENT FOR COOPERATION
BETWEEN
DENMARK, FINLAND, ICELAND, NORWAY, AND SWEDEN
[March 23, 1962]

The governments of Denmark, Finland, Iceland, Norway, and Sweden, desirous of developing further the close unity that exists among the Nordic nations in matters cultural, conceptions of law and society, and wanting to carry forward cooperation among the people of the North;

striving for uniform rules and regulations among the four nations over the widest possible areas;

desiring to achieve, in all fields where opportunities therefor exist, expedient and practical division of labor among the five countries;

and desiring to continue the cooperation important to all our nations, within the Nordic Council and other organs of cooperation,

have agreed to the following.

## Introductory Provision

ARTICLE 1. The signatories shall attempt to preserve and develop further cooperation between themselves in the field of legal matters, in cultural, social, and economic areas, as well as in matters relating to traffic.

## Cooperation in Legal Matters

ARTICLE 2. The contracting parties shall continue to work for the establishment of the greatest possible legal equality between the citizens of a Nordic country who reside in another Nordic country, and the citizens of the country where they reside.

ARTICLE 3. The contracting parties shall attempt to make it easier for citizens of one Nordic country to acquire citizenship in another.

ARTICLE 4. The contracting parties shall continue their cooperation in matters pertaining to law in order to achieve the greatest possible uniformity in the field of civil law.

131

ARTICLE 5. The contracting parties should strive for uniform provisions regarding crimes and punishments therefor. It should be possible, over a wide range of cases, to investigate and prosecute crimes committed in one Nordic country even in another Nordic country.

ARTICLE 6. The contracting parties should attempt, even in areas other than the ones mentioned, to achieve coordination in legislation whenever coordination seems to serve a useful purpose.

ARTICLE 7. Each contracting party should endeavor to bring about regulations which permit the carrying out of one Nordic nation's court verdicts, or decisions by some other authority, within the jurisdiction of the other signatories.

### Cultural Cooperation

ARTICLE 8. In each of the Nordic countries, the teaching and instruction given in schools should include, in appropriate degree, instruction in the languages of the other Nordic nations, as well as instruction concerning their culture and general social conditions.

ARTICLE 9. Each signatory should maintain and expand, in its educational institutions, opportunities for study, and for taking examinations, for students from the other Nordic countries. Preliminary examinations passed in one country should be accepted, to the greatest possible extent, toward meeting final examination requirements in another.

Fellowship and scholarship aid should be granted without reference to the country where studies are pursued.

ARTICLE 10. The contracting parties should introduce such uniformity in their public instruction as is intended to afford competence in a given trade. Such instruction should be recognized as giving, as far as possible, the same competence in all of the Nordic countries. If special national considerations require it, additional training might, however, be required.

ARTICLE 11. In areas where cooperation will serve useful purposes, the development of educational establishments should be coordinated by means of continuing cooperation in planning and execution.

ARTICLE 12. In the field of research, cooperation should be directed in a manner that will coordinate and assure the most effective use of available funds and other resources, *inter alia* by establishing common institutions.

ARTICLE 13. In order to support and strengthen cultural development, the signatories shall support the free education of the people, as well as to foster exchanges within the areas of literature, art, music, the theater, the moving pictures, and other fields of cultural endeavor. The possibilities offered by radio and television should therewith be utilized.

ARTICLE 14. The signatories should preserve and expand further the common Nordic labor market, along the lines drawn by earlier agreements. Labor exchanges and vocational guidance should be coordinated;

the exchange of trainees should be free. Attempts should be made to render uniform the national rules and provisions regarding the protection of workers and such-like matters.

ARTICLE 15. The signatories should labor to the end that the citizen of a Nordic country, while residing in another, will enjoy to the fullest possible extent the social benefits available to the natives.

ARTICLE 16. The signatories shall develop further their cooperation in the fields of health, the care of the sick, children, and youth, as well as efforts on behalf of temperance.

ARTICLE 17. Each signatory should strive for a medical, technical, and such-like system of inspection and control in a manner that certification in one country can be accepted in the other Nordic countries.

*Economic Cooperation*

ARTICLE 18. The contracting parties shall, in order to promote economic cooperation in various fields, discuss questions dealing with economic policy. Attention should be given therewith to the possibility of coordinating measures intended to stabilize business conditions.

ARTICLE 19. It is the intention of the signatories to promote, as extensively as possible, cooperation between their countries in the areas of production and investment, and in this connection to create favorable circumstances for direct cooperation between enterprises active in two or more of the Nordic countries. In their effort to develop further their cooperation, as part of large international cooperation, they should strive for a practical division of labor, among themselves, in matters of production and investment.

ARTICLE 20. The signatories shall labor for the greatest possible freedom for the movement of capital between the Nordic countries. Attempts will be made to find common solutions for other payments and foreign-exchange problems that interest them all.

ARTICLE 21. The signatories will endeavor to strengthen existing cooperation designed to remove obstacles to trade between the Nordic countries, and agree to develop and strengthen this cooperation as far as possible.

ARTICLE 22. The signatories shall attempt to promote, each for himself and also together, Nordic interests when international commercial questions are involved.

ARTICLE 23. The contracting parties shall endeavor to coordinate the technical and administrative customs regulations and to bring about such simplification of customs arrangements as will contribute to easier traffic between them.

ARTICLE 24. Regulation trade in the areas adjacent to the boundaries shall be such as to cause the least possible trouble to the inhabitants.

ARTICLE 25. Whenever necessary and when the essential prerequisites for the economic development of the areas close to the border belonging to two or more signatories exist, they will attempt to cooperate in promoting such development.

### Cooperation in the Area of Traffic and Communication

ARTICLE 26. The contracting parties shall attempt to expand the cooperation that already exists between them in the field of traffic and communication and will attempt to develop it in order to improve connections and the exchange of goods between them, and in order to solve the problems that still may exist in this area.

ARTICLE 27. The development of traffic connections involving the territory of two or more of the contracting parties shall be undertaken on the basis of consultation between the parties concerned.

ARTICLE 28. The signatories shall attempt to retain and develop further the cooperation which has turned their territories into a single passport-control area. The control of travelers who cross the borders of the Nordic countries shall be further simplified and rendered uniform.

ARTICLE 29. The signatories will coordinate the efforts to increase the safety of traffic.

### Other Forms of Cooperation

ARTICLE 30. Whenever possible and practical, the contracting parties shall consult with each other regarding questions of common interest that are considered in international organizations and at international conferences.

ARTICLE 31. A foreign-service officer of a signatory who is serving abroad, outside the Nordic countries, shall assist, insofar as it is in keeping with his responsibilities in discharging his duties, citizens of another Nordic country if it lacks representation in the area in question.

ARTICLE 32. The contracting parties shall coordinate, whenever it is possible and practical, their efforts to aid and to work with underdeveloped countries.

ARTICLE 33. Measures intended to publicize and to increase knowledge of the Nordic countries and Nordic cooperation should be undertaken in close cooperation between the contracting parties and their informational organization abroad. Whenever convenient, the five countries should act and appear together.

ARTICLE 34. The contracting parties shall endeavor to render uniform the various branches of their official statistical services.

### The Forms of Nordic Cooperation

ARTICLE 35. In order to achieve the purposes mentioned in this agreement, the contracting parties shall continue to consult one another and, when necessary, undertake action in common.

This cooperation shall take place, as has been the case hitherto, at meetings of cabinet members, within the framework of the Nordic Council and its organs, according to the directives of the Statute of the Council, and in various other organizations for cooperation, or between appropriate officials.

ARTICLE 36. The Nordic Council shall be given an opportunity to express itself regarding the principles of Nordic cooperation except when, because of the time element, this is not possible.

ARTICLE 37. Accords that have been entered into as the result of the cooperation of two or more of the contracting parties cannot be changed by one party, except upon notice to the others. Notice is not required, however, in matters requiring quick action, or are of no particular importance.

ARTICLE 38. The authorities and officials of the Nordic countries may correspond with each other in regard to matters other than those which, because of their nature or other reasons, must be handled by and through the Ministry for Foreign Affairs.

ARTICLE 39. This agreement will be ratified and the instruments of ratification shall be deposited, as soon as possible, with the Ministry for Foreign Affairs of Finland.

The Agreement becomes effective on the first day of the month following the deposit of ratifications by all of the contracting parties.

ARTICLE 40. [The agreement can be cancelled upon written notice, given to the Government of Finland, and becomes effective six months after notice.]

In witness whereof [we have] signed this agreement,

Signed in Helsinki, in one copy done in Danish, Finnish, Icelandic, Norwegian, and Swedish, each of which text is equally authentic, the twenty-third of March nineteen hundred and sixty-two.

[Signatures]

## SUGGESTED READINGS

The bibliographical suggestions that follow are limited to works in English. There were two reasons for not including books or other contributions in the Scandinavian languages. First, the languages of the North are less well-known outside Scandinavia than they deserve to be. Second, historical works and other literature in English dealing with Scandinavia has grown gratifyingly during the past three or four decades. Although some of it has been authored by writers short on fact and long on good intentions, much of it offers dependable guidance to an understanding of the past history and present circumstances of the peoples of the North. As might be expected, most of the works in English have been written by foreign observers or students. Some of them have been persuaded, either by personal inclination or chance circumstance, to interpret the Scandinavian lands in an uncritical manner. The reader will therefore find many discussions of the cooperatives, the "planned society," the virtues of the "middle way," the advantages of "controlled" economies, and of politics and government allegedly free from the deficiencies found in countries less favored by a discriminating Providence. Such discussions often imply that the Scandinavians have devised formulae for solving society's ills that are not only successfully applied in the North but are also available to other lands sensible enough to appropriate and make use of them. It is fortunate that works in this category are balanced by other contributions content to understand and describe rather than to exhort and prescribe.

OFFICIAL PUBLICATIONS. A good many official and semiofficial publications useful to students are available. Each of the Scandinavian countries publishes an annual Statistical Yearbook, with an English text and explanations. A number of special publications also deserve mention. *Denmark*, published in 1961 by the Royal Danish Ministry of Foreign Affairs (and earlier versions of the same work), is an excellent compilation, as is the *Danish Foreign Office Journal*. Equally useful are the *Norway Yearbook* and *Introduction to Finland, 1963*, and *News of Norway* issued by the Norwegian Information Service in Washington, D.C. Publications bearing the imprimatur of the Swedish Institute (Svenska

Institutet) in Stockholm offer a many-sided coverage of the economic, political, and social aspects of Sweden and its people. The leading Scandinavian banks and other important economic interests have long published monthly and quarterly surveys in English that open up vistas well beyond mere banking matters. (The *Quarterly Review* of the Skandinaviska Banken in Stockholm or the Bank of Finland *Monthly Bulletin* are excellent illustrations of these surveys.) Several of these publications are available at the information bureaus or other offices maintained abroad by the Scandinavian governments.

GENERAL HISTORIES. There is no general history of Scandinavia, although several surveys of special aspects of Scandinavian development have appeared, particularly since the end of World War II. Of the histories of the individual countries, the following works are especially helpful. DENMARK: John Henry S. Birch, *Denmark in History* (London, 1938); John Danstrup, *A History of Denmark* (Copenhagen, 1949); Viggo Starcke, *Denmark in World History* (Copenhagen, 1962). FINLAND: Eino K. I. Jutikkala, *A History of Finland* (New York, 1962); John H. Wuorinen, *A History of Finland* (New York, 1965) and *Nationalism in Modern Finland* (New York, 1931). ICELAND: Knut Gjerset, *History of Iceland* (New York, 1924); Amy E. Jensen, *Iceland: Old-New Republic* (New York, 1954). NORWAY: Thomas K. Derry, *A Short History of Norway* (London, 1957); Knut Gjerset, *History of the Norwegian People* (2 vols., New York, 1916, 1932); Karen Larsen, *A History of Norway* (Princeton, N.J., 1948). SWEDEN: Ingvar Anderson, *A History of Sweden* (New York, 1956); Carl Hallendorff and Adolf Schuck, *History of Sweden* (Stockholm, 1929); Eli F. Heckscher, *An Economic History of Sweden*, translated by Goran Ohlin (Cambridge, Mass., 1954); Andrew A. Stomberg, *A History of Sweden* (New York, 1931).

A work that stands in a category by itself is *Scandinavia, Past and Present*, edited by Jorgen Bukdahl, *et al.* (3 vols., Copenhagen, 1959). Scores of Scandinavian scholars contributed to its 270-odd chapters. Approximately half its 2146 pages are devoted to the relatively recent past or to the contemporary scene. Although somewhat fragmentary in organization these volumes contain much valuable information. Despite its title, Franklin D. Scott's excellent *The United States and Scandinavia* (Cambridge, Mass., 1950) is almost wholly devoted to Scandinavia. Three substantial chapters summarize the developments after 1939. W. R. Mead, *An Economic Geography of the Scandinavian States and Finland* (London, 1958) is indispensable for the broad area it covers.

Articles on Scandinavian history, economic and cultural developments, and foreign affairs appear regularly in the *American-Scandinavian Review*, a quarterly published since 1913 by the American Scandinavian Foundation; the *American-Swedish Monthly*, published by the Swedish Chamber of Commerce of the United States; the *Danish Foreign Office Journal* (already mentioned), published by the Danish Ministry for Foreign

Affairs; *Norwegian-American Commerce*, published by the Norwegian American Chamber of Commerce; and the Bank of Finland *Monthly Bulletin*. Scandinavian topics are less frequently discussed in *Foreign Affairs*, *World Affairs*, *The Journal of International Affairs*, the *Annals* of the American Academy of Political and Social Science, the *Scandinavian Economic History Review* (published in Stockholm), and *World Politics*. *Current History* has published articles on Scandinavia with fair regularity since the early 1950s.

ECONOMIC AND SOCIAL DEVELOPMENTS. The broad range of development and concerns ranging, say, from basic aspects of national economy to programs of social welfare legislation has been recorded in a surprisingly large number of works, especially since the 1930s. The economies of the five nations were described and analyzed by the Scandinavian Delegations for Economic Cooperation in *The Northern Countries in World Economy* (published in the Scandinavian capitals in 1937). William C. Chamberlin, *The Economic Development of Iceland Through World War II* (New York, 1947); Eli F. Hechscher, *An Economic History of Sweden* (Cambridge, Mass., 1954); Conrad Hofgaard (ed.), *Norway, A Survey of Exports and Economic Developments* (Oslo, 1948); Arthur F. Montgomery, *The Rise of Modern Industry in Sweden* (London, 1939) and *How Sweden Overcame the Depression* (Stockholm, 1938); Christopher L. Paus, *Report on Economic and Commercial Conditions in Norway* (London, 1938); Bruno Suviranta, *Finland's War Indemnity* (Stockholm, 1947); and *The Scandinavian States and Finland: A Political and Economic Survey*, published in London in 1951 by the Royal Institute of International Affairs, go a long way toward sketching the essential contours of the economies of the North.

The cooperative movement in Scandinavia has attracted considerable attention, especially since the publication of Marquis W. Child's well-intentioned *Sweden: The Middle Way* in 1936. More realistic appraisals are found in Henning Ravnholt, *The Danish Cooperative Movement* (Copenhagen, 1947); Anders Hedberg, *Consumers' Cooperation in Sweden* (Stockholm 1948); T. Ohde, *Finland: A Nation of Cooperators*, translated by John Downie (London, 1931). Social problems, policies, and purposes are described in O. B. Grimley, *The New Norway* (Oslo, 1937); John Eric Nordskog, *Social Reform in Norway* (Los Angeles, 1935); Peter Manniche, *Denmark: A Social Laboratory* (Copenhagen, 1939); I. Laati, *Social Legislation and Activity in Finland* (Helsinki, 1939); John Graham, Jr., *Housing in Scandinavia* (Chapel Hill, N.C., 1940); Walter Galenson, *Labor in Norway* (Cambridge, Mass., 1949); James J. Robbins, *The Government of Labor Relations in Sweden* (Chapel Hill, N.C., 1942); Leonard Silk, *Sweden Plans for Better Housing* (Durham, N.C., 1948); John H. Wuorinen, *The Prohibition Experiment in Finland* (New York, 1931).

GOVERNMENT AND POLITICS. The fascinating record of Scandinavian politics and government is presented in a number of studies. Some of them suffer from the effort to describe "functioning democracy" in terms that idealize rather than delineate the realities of the workaday world. The following works, although they do not offer fully systematic treatment of the subject, describe a wide range of pertinent fact and circumstance. Nils Andrén, *Modern Swedish Government* (Stockholm, 1961); Ben A. Arnesen, *The Democratic Monarchies of Scandinavia* (New York, 1949); Margaret Cole and Charles Smith (eds.), *Democratic Sweden* (New York, 1939); Arvid Enckell, *Democratic Finland* (London, 1948); Finnish Political Science Association, *Democracy in Finland* (Helsinki, 1960); Elis W. Håstad, *The Parliament of Sweden* (London, 1957); Nils Herlitz, *Sweden: A Modern Democracy on Ancient Foundations* (Minneapolis, Minn., 1939); J. A. Lauwerys (ed.), *Scandinavian Democracy* (Copenhagen, 1958); P. Manniche, *Living Democracy in Denmark* (Copenhagen, 1952); Dankwart A. Rustow, *The Politics of Compromise: A Study of Parties and Cabinet Government in Sweden* (Princeton, N.J., 1955); James Storring, *Norwegian Democracy* (New York, 1963).

FOREIGN POLICY AND AFFAIRS. The literature in English dealing with Scandinavian foreign policy—as the term is used in its widest sense—is gratifyingly extensive. This is perhaps not surprising. The antecedents of the last war seemed, after 1945, to require close re-examination. The war itself meant the gravest of dangers to the independence of these nations, and its aftermath heavily accented the concerns and complicated the problems of national safety and progress. Finland attacked by Russia, Denmark and Norway invaded and occupied by Germany, Iceland under the friendly military occupation of the Western Allies, and Sweden, favored by good fortune, remaining neutral during the war—all provided ample reason after 1945 for description, explanation and justification of the record of each nation during the trying years. Not a little of the explanation and justification was addressed, understandably, to the English-speaking world. The following works cover the main aspects of general foreign policy; the individual titles suffice to indicate the special area covered. Samuel Abrahamsen, *Sweden's Foreign Policy* (Washington, D.C., 1957); Eric C. Bellquist, *Some Aspects of the Recent Foreign Policy of Sweden* (Berkeley, Calif., 1929); Finnish Political Science Association, *Finnish Foreign Policy* (Helsinki, 1963); Annette Baker Fox, *The Power of Small States: Diplomacy in World War II* (Chicago, 1959); Max Jakobson, *The Diplomacy of the Winter War: An Account of the Russo-Finnish Conflict, 1939-40* (Cambridge, Mass., 1961); Shepard Jones, *The Scandinavian States and the League of Nations* (Princeton, N.J., 1929); Rowland Kenny, *The Northern Tangle: Scandinavia and the Postwar World* (London, 1946); Donald E. Nuechterlein, *Iceland: Reluctant Ally* (Ithaca, N.Y., 1961); Max Sorensen and Niels J. Haagerup, *Denmark and the United Nations* (New York, 1956); Herbert Tingsten, *The Debate on the Foreign Policy of Sweden 1919-39.*
To these studies should be added a number of books specifically deal-

ing with the years 1939-45. Monica Curtis (ed.), *Documents on International Affairs: Norway and the War, September 1939-December 1940* (London, 1941); Thomas K. Derry, *The Campaign in Norway* (London, 1952); Ministry for Foreign Affairs (Helsinki), *Finland Reveals Her Secret Documents on Soviet Policy, March 1940-June 1941* (New York, 1941); Carl J. Hambro, *I Saw It Happen in Norway* (New York, 1941); Bjarne Hoye and Trygve M. Ager, *The Fight of the Norwegian Church Against Nazism* (New York, 1943); Halvdan Koht, *Norway: Neutral and Invaded* (New York, 1941); D. Lemkul, *Journey to London: The Story of the Norwegian Government at War* (London, 1945); C. Leonard Lundin, *Finland in the Second World War* (Bloomington, Ind., 1957); Carl Gustaf Mannerheim, *Memoirs of Marshal Mannerheim* (London, 1953); Borge Outze, *Denmark During the German Occupation* (Copenhagen, 1946); Vaino Tanner, *The Winter War* (Stanford, Calif., 1957); Jacob S. Worm-Muller, *Norway Revolts Against the Nazis* (London, 1941); John H. Wuorinen (ed.), *Finland and World War II, 1939-44* (New York, 1948).

SCANDINAVIAN COOPERATION. Increasing Scandinavian cooperation, especially since 1945, has been extensively recorded and discussed. Nearly all of the discussion is, however, in the Scandinavian languages, and no up-to-date comprehensive survey in English has yet been published. An early phase of the problem is presented by Raymond E. Lindgren in *Norway-Sweden: Union, Disunion, and Scandinavian Integration* (Princeton, N.J., 1959). John H. Wuorinen's chapter on "Scandinavia and the Rise of Modern National Consciousness," in Edward Mead Earle (ed.), *Nationalism and Internationalism* (New York, 1950), summarizes some of the ideological considerations relating to the subject. Frants W. Wendt's *The Nordic Council and Cooperation in Scandinavia* (Copenhagen, 1959), offers an adequate survey of the first five years of the Council. The following articles discuss various phases of the question: Hans Hedtoft, "The Nordic Council," *The American Scandinavian Review* (March 1954); Norman J. Padelford, "Regional Cooperation in Scandinavia," *International Organization* (Autumn 1957); Gunnar C. Wasberg, "The Nordic Cultural Commission," *The American-Scandinavian Review* (June 1961); Lyman B. Burbank, "Scandinavian Integration and Western Defense," *Foreign Affairs* (October 1956); and the articles by John H. Wuorinen: "Problems of the Scandinavian Bloc," *Current History* (January 1949); "Scandinavian Unity: Problems and Prospects," *The American-Scandinavian Review* (Autumn 1957); "Russia, Scandinavia, and the Baltic States," *Current History* (February 1955); "Neutralism in Scandinavia," *ibid.* (November 1955); "Scandinavian Foreign Policy Problems: Recent Trends and Emerging Prospects," *The American-Scandinavian Review* (June 1960); "Scandinavia and West Europe Today," *Current History* (December 1964).

# INDEX

141

## The Modern Nations in Historical Perspective